gardens by design ❧ THE NATIONAL TRUST

old roses

GRAHAM MURPHY

To Suzanne and Trevor,
Brenda and Sophie

First published in 2003 by
National Trust Enterprises Ltd
36 Queen Anne's Gate, London SW1H 9AS

www.nationaltrust.org.uk

Cataloguing in Publication Data is available from the British
Library

ISBN 0 7078 0354 3

Designed by Barbara Mercer
Colour origination by Digital Imaging Ltd
Printed and bound in Hong Kong by Printing Express Ltd

Front cover: 'Madame Isaac Pereire'. A Parisian
nurseryman saw the potential of this rose but it
was despised by show-judges for being a plant of
ungainly appearance. Today it is widely recognised
as one of the finest old-fashioned 'climbing' roses
with superb fragrance.

Back cover: *Rosa glauca*. A wild rose of the
Pyrenees that has proved invaluable in gardening
and floristry for the colour of its glaucus foliage.
The fleeting flowers – clear pink fading to white
around the light-yellow stamens – give way to
bunches of reddish-purple hips.

Page 1: A close-up of 'Général Jacqueminot'
petals. Once the height of fashion in Paris and
New York, these rich-crimson perfumed flowers
were considered the best in floristry before the
introduction of scentless modern red roses.

Page 2: 'Gloire de France': One of 300 or so
surviving examples of the fragrant Gallica Roses
of the early nineteenth century. This low-growing
cultivar (1.2m) produces fully double pale pink
flowers with a deeper coloured centre. The petals
reflex to form a delightful soft pink pompon.

Contents

Introduction: *The Rose in History*

Of the many plants that are cultivated, the rose is the most popular. No other flower has the power to convey such a variety of our most intimate feelings. A rose can communicate love, sympathy, loyalty, or simply the delight that we share when someone is blessed and has cause to feel happy. Civilisations throughout the world have cherished roses for their beauty of colour and fragrance, much as we do today, for their ability to crown happiness at times of human achievement, to bring serenity at times of distress. In 2002, during the service held at St Paul's Cathedral, London, to commemorate the victims of the terrorist attacks on the USA on 11 September 2001, 3,000 rose petals – representing the number of people who lost their lives – were dropped onto the congregation.

'Gipsy Boy'. A semi-double deep crimson Bourbon Rose raised in the Geschwind nursery, Hungary, early last century. The shrub is tall (1.8m) and dense with arching stems, becoming a mass of flowers in mid-summer.

(*Opposite*): 'Magna Carta'. Fully double, fragrant, cupped flowers, clear pink with dark veining, in bloom amid Canterbury Bells in the gardens of Mottisfont Abbey, Hampshire. 'Magna Carta' is a Hybrid Perpetual Rose introduced in 1876 by William Paul, the most skilful plantsman in Victorian England.

For centuries the extracts of rose flowers, absorbed in oils and unguents, were used as perfumes throughout the East and the lands of the Mediterranean at festivals and ceremonies. Garlands of roses were placed, along with phials of aromatic oils, in the tombs of ancient Egypt; frescoes depict how, with fine clothes and jewellery, sweet-scented pomades of perfume were worn at banquets and state occasions.

For the ancient Greeks, the rose was both a wild shrub and a garden plant. They took delight in its complex beauty and made it an object of scientific inquiry, comparing it with other plants and defining its variety by the number of its petals. By the time of Roman domination of the Greek World, cultivation of roses was a major industry: rose flower-heads were harvested on a massive scale, to be thrown in the path of processions and scattered in clouds from portals in the ceilings of banqueting halls onto the guests below. Meetings of military or political importance were conducted beneath the rose to remind those present of the need for discretion.

Introduction

At first there was some reaction against the rose among Christians, deriving from its association with the decadence of pagan Rome. This hostility, however, lacked conviction. While some of the Church Fathers banned wreaths and crowns of roses and lilies, others took the rose to be a symbol of sanctity, its beauty indicative of paradise. The Latin Lyric, 'Lay of the Little Bird', shows that the rose was never entirely out of favour:

> So sweet was the savour of roses and other flowers
> and simples that sick persons, borne in the garden in
> a litter, walked forth sound and well for having passed
> the night in so lovely a place.

The healing properties of plants in the herb garden are so magnified here that cures occur without the skill of apothecaries and therefore seem attributable to divine power alone.

In 794 the Emperor Charlemagne ordained the planting of roses and lilies in all gardens on land controlled by the Crown. The monk Alcuin, who left his monastery in York to join the Emperor's court, is thought to have influenced him in the drafting of this decree. Throughout the medieval period monks cherished the rose as 'the guardian' of their herb plots. As he took leave of his cell Alcuin wrote:

> Thy cloisters smell of apple trees in the gardens and
> white lilies mingle with little red roses.

For his own use, Charlemagne had imported rose perfume from Persia where attar, a form of rose oil, had long been the most traditional and expensive of marriage gifts. The growing of roses and the extraction of rose oil became a major industry there. This product of the region of Shiraz not only went westward but was taken eastward by the Arabs into India and used both as a perfume and a libation at festivals: the red dye sprayed on the devotees of Krishna is even now, by tradition, first mixed with rose-water.

In China also, rose petals were a source of fragrance, mixed with other flower-heads and the leaves of fine herbs. Musk, extracted from the native deer, was the most prized of all substances for the making of pomanders. It was customary to use a minute amount of this otherwise heavy, sweet and repugnantly strong odour, to counteract the evanescence of floral ingredients. Perfume was important to establish good social relations, and Chinese books of etiquette warn the reader never to forget to 'bind a sachet of scent to the girdle'.

Rather than import attar from Persia, apothecaries in France in the thirteenth century established rose-oil manufacture in the town of Provins, south-east of Paris. Fields were given over to *Rosa gallica* var. *officinalis*, the Apothecary's Rose (see p.78). Such intensive cultivation no doubt assisted the development of varieties, the number of which increased enormously due to extensive horticulture in the Low Countries during the seventeenth and eighteenth centuries. Dutch hybridisation of the most ancient classes of roses prepared the way for a golden age of rose-growing in France, in the early part of the nineteenth century.

The new varieties of roses were introduced throughout northern Europe and settlers of the New World took them across the Atlantic. Old colonial cemeteries are now the hunting ground of 'rose rustlers' seeking to recover varieties that have long been lost, as a favourite rose would often be planted in memory of a loved one. This is not to say that roses were not indigenous to that continent. Legends of the Native Americans convey a deep respect for the natural world, its creatures and plants, including varieties of the wild rose, *Rosa carolina*. One such legend describes how a Cherokee warrior's sweetheart was spared from an enemy raid by being magically transformed into a single white rose. She

Rosa gallica var. *officinalis*: The ancient and very fragrant Apothecary's Rose, so-called because of the use of its petals in confections, medicines and cleansing rose-water. The profuse light crimson flowers last only a few weeks, but are superseded by attractive oval hips. The perfect rose for a herb garden.

9

later gained thorns to prevent her from being crushed beneath her careless lover's feet.

In literature and art, the rose has long been used as a central image. In *Beauty and the Beast*, a daughter's request for a rose triggers the events leading to her father being taken hostage. Only when Beauty marries the Beast to secure her father's freedom does her bravery and love turn the Beast into a handsome prince. In many cultures the rose is a symbol of the constancy of love, not least in Persia, where generations of artists depict the flower as the only fit suitor for the nightingale:

> You may place a hundred handfuls of fragrant herbs and
> flowers before the Nightingale; yet he wishes not, in his
> constant heart, for more than the sweet breath of his
> beloved Rose.

Not all associations of ideas with the rose are so positive. Shakespeare makes more than fifty references to the flower. Among the most poignant are those which occur in his dramatisation of the War of the Roses, the dreadful and bloody conflict between the Houses of York and Lancaster. Here the rose is stylised in an heraldic badge, an emblem for purposes of war: the white *Rosa alba* for York and the red *Rosa gallica officinalis* for Lancaster.

Most other ancient usages of the symbol opine a more positive message, the one common to children's tales – that suffering bravely borne nurses the hope of redemption. In the tradition of the Christian martyrs, the single-flower red rose, with its five petals, reminds the believer of the five wounds of Christ and his passion, the gateway to Heaven.

By the nineteenth century, the rose was no longer a potent symbol of theology. The identification of varieties by the attribution of famous names was, for France at least, the equivalent of the New Year's Honours list in the UK. Not everyone proved worthy of their citation and in many cases their story was quickly forgotten. As varieties proliferated the rose lost much of its mystery and, with advances in the science of medicine, its privileged place in the art of healing.

Old Roses After 1800

A decline in the popularity of the oldest roses began in the Victorian age. Roses brought from China, when crossed with European varieties, created new classes which the public much preferred for their longer period of flowering. The 1840 nursery catalogue of Paul & Son of Cheshunt, Hertfordshire, listed 292 cultivars of Alba, Gallica, Damask and Centifolia roses. By 1865 the number in these oldest classes was reduced to 51, many would be lost forever. In France, the 1829 catalogue of Desportes lists 1,213 Gallicas: today we know of about 300.

By far the most numerous new breed of rose was the Hybrid Perpetual. In the 1820s such roses barely existed, but by 1872 Paul's catalogue listed 538. Towards the end of the century across Europe and in America there were in excess of 3,000 cultivars in this class, the roses of previous centuries having been almost totally eclipsed. However, Hybrid Perpetuals were themselves destined for the nursery bonfire and many had already reached its flames before the close of the Victorian era. They were being ousted by our modern roses, the more colourful but often brash Hybrid Teas.

Just how fickle the market could be is illustrated by the history of 'Général Jacqueminot' (see p.54), a rose introduced in France in 1853. Within a couple of decades it had spread throughout Europe and America. As a Hybrid Perpetual, 'Général Jacqueminot'

'Gloire de Ducher' in October: A Hybrid Perpetual rose, fragrant and deep purple-crimson, introduced by the nursery of Veuve Ducher at Lyons, in 1865. Summer flowers on side shoots give way to large blooms at the end of the new shoots in autumn, a good rose for 'pegging down' (see p.52).

was not only occupying the space once reserved for the old Gallicas but also creating for itself a whole new industry. Such was the demand for this rose that, in addition to nursery fields, it took up an estimated 18,400 square metres under glass in the region of New York alone. Horticulturist writers are not often given to hyperbole, but T.B. Jenkins claimed it had 'slept on the bosom of every belle'. In the days approaching Christmas 'the only Jacqueminot buds to be found in the city were sold for 15 dollars each or eight times their weight in gold'. In Pittsburgh and elsewhere it was a similar story.

'Général Jacqueminot' has fortunately survived the decimation since wrought upon its class. In David Austin's catalogue it now languishes on the supplementary list. Ironically, however, some of the roses it once threatened are among the main features. The oldest roses are coming back into fashion.

As the Hybrid Perpetuals swept through Victorian England, manuals were published for the benefit of enthusiasts. William Paul's *The Rose Garden* (1848) for the experts, and seventeen editions of Dean Reynolds Hole's *Book about Roses* (1869) for the general reader. Hole was the impresario of rose exhibitions, a promoter of the first National Rose Show and a founder in 1876 of the National Rose Society. Tennyson hailed him as 'the Rose King'.

For amateur enthusiasts from all walks of

'Ardoisée de Lyons': One of the finest Hybrid Perpetual Roses, introduced by the nursery of Damaizin in 1858. The fully double and quartered flowers are rich cerise shaded violet and purple, with a rich perfume.

'Phyllis Bide': A Multiflora
Rambler raised in England in
1923. This rose will grow to
between 3 and 4 metres and
flower continuously throughout
summer and late into autumn.
The flowers are scented,
double, and clear yellow flushed
pink.

society, growing Hybrid Perpetuals and new Hybrid Teas – the shows, the cups, the medals and the prizes – became so important that their gardens resembled nursery trials fields. The son of Foster-Melliar, another clerical author (*The Book of the Rose*, 1894), said of his father that 'what he liked best of all was to have a single perfect rose in a specimen glass by itself. He would not step a yard to see banks of roses, arches of roses, hedges of roses'.

In the late 1890s the work of the great English gardener, Gertrude Jekyll (1843–1932), challenged this obsession with indoor show. While a student at Kensington Art School, she studied how William Morris had used the arching stems of wild roses for designs on hand-printed linen. In the company of the young architect Edwin Lutyens, she toured the lanes of rural Surrey seeking out ideal forms of old roses and other flowers, largely neglected, growing by old walls and in cottage gardens. In the midst of an agricultural depression and abject rural poverty there was no shortage of romantic dereliction in the countryside.

Suffering the rapid onset of myopia, Jekyll was obliged to give up fine art and chose to become a landscape gardener. 'Painting with a pole' is how she thought of her new career. Unconvinced by many aspects of formal garden design, she found an ally in the Irish horticulturist, William Robinson, the advocate of a wild style. Robinson's mission was to be rid of flowerbeds, which he saw as possessing 'the lifeless and offensive formality of wallpaper and carpet'. He preferred 'an epitome of the great flower garden of the world itself'. In *Roses for English Gardens*, (1902), written in collaboration with the renowned rose-grower Gerard Mawley, Jekyll opens with chapters extolling the use of roses on pillars and swags, on pergolas and arches, over walls and against walls, as scramblers over eyesores, 'as fountains growing free … converting ugliness to beauty'.

Gertrude Jekyll designed the planting in over 300 gardens in Europe and America, many within layouts and accompanying house plans by Lutyens. For roses to achieve the effects she desired, she found it necessary to resort to the old cultivars and Ramblers. The legacy of her style has been to secure a place for old roses in the design of modern gardens for the foreseeable future.

Although old roses are unable to compete with the wider range of colours and extended show of the modern Hybrid Teas, they are now planted where the need arises for a rose with vigour, often capable of resisting pests and disease. Ellen Willmott's *The Genus Rosa* (1914) served as a reference work for wild and old varieties as nurserymen like Tom Smith of Newry and, later, Graham Stuart Thomas at Sunningdale in Berkshire began rebuilding stocks of the old classes. Inspired by the enthusiast Edward Bunyard's *Old Garden Roses* (1936), Thomas toured gardens in England and Ireland, and then sent abroad for as many of the very old and early Victorian varieties as could be found in Europe and America. The crowning achievement of his work as Gardens Adviser to the National Trust was to establish a National Collection of Old Roses in the gardens of Mottisfont Abbey in Hampshire. For lovers of old roses, *The Graham Stuart Thomas Rose Book* (1994) is nothing short of a bible.

A chance meeting between Thomas and David Austin, on a tour of the Paris rosaries in the 1950s, confirmed the latter's determination to start a new breed of shrub roses. These combine old rose shape and fragrance and soft colours with an extended period of flowering and are known as The English Roses. Soon after Austin established his trials fields at Albrighton, Shropshire, Peter Beale, the author of *Classic Roses* (1985), began collecting all manner of old roses for sale to the public at his nursery in Attleborough, Norfolk. The best of the Victorian roses were also coming back into fashion.

The Classes of Old Roses

Roses have been evolving naturally on earth for 35 million years and have only relatively recently come into cultivation. They were probably cared for by gardeners in China some 5,000 years ago. Herodotus, the fifth-century Greek historian, was clearly captivated by what gardening can do. He described the gardens of Midas, son of Gordias, 'in which [once] wild roses grew, each one having sixty petals, surpassing all others in fragrance'. A century later, Plato's pupil Theophrastus, the father of botany, was no less amazed that 'some have five, some have twelve or twenty, some have even a hundred petals'. The encyclopaedist Pliny, writing in the first century AD, listed twelve roses, ten of which were named according to their place of origin in the world as the Romans knew it. Just two were identified by their appearance, the thorn rose and the rose of a hundred petals, which is not, however, the rose we now call a Centifolia. Centifolias seem to have been the culmination of the crossbreeding of five ancient roses which, according to the histories of Dutch horticulture, produced more than 200 varieties in the seventeenth century.

An obscure poetic text by Franeau, *Le Jardin d'Hyuer* (Douai, 1616), is perhaps the first clear division of roses into four classes:

La Rose de Provence est la mieux odorante	(Centifolia)
La Rose Pestanois est deux fois florissante …	(Damask)
La Rose pure blanche est assez ordinaire	(Alba)
Mais la passe velours n'est point si populaire	(Gallica)

These four classes – Albas, Gallicas, Damasks and Centifolias – are today renowned for their fragrance, their exquisite flowers and a distinctive range of colour from white to deep pink and purple. Rather than associate them with modern roses, we need to think of these old roses as somewhat special garden shrubs. They are tough plants, which flower for a short time and can be used in a variety of ways. However, not everyone will want to grow the oldest roses; many of us can appreciate them simply by access to gardens in late June and early July, where there may be just one or two, or an entire collection of them.

Of Alba roses there are now less than 25 varieties, their flowers are in the range of pink to white and sweetly scented. Their thorns, bark, leaves and hips betray their kinship to the Dog Roses (see p.76) from which they are derived, these wildlings having hybridised with a Damask rose. Albas grow strongly from the base and form a thicket of branches above; the shoots of this top growth need to be cut back a little after flowering. The removal of two-thirds of the length of the very long stems is carried out in winter.

Alba roses have been known to survive in gardens for a hundred years or more despite disturbances of the ground and diseases and pests which see off most other flowers. Tolerant of partial shade, they will grow fairly well on a north wall and extremely well in a flowerbed, where their grey-green leaves and pale blooms blend with almost any planting scheme. The variety best known for its pure fragrance is 'Great Maiden's Blush' ('Cuisse de Nymphe', see p.32); for the finest flower, 'Königin von Dänemark' (see p.60). In Botticelli's most famous painting, *The Birth of Venus*, we see Alba roses descending in showers. According to legend, Venus rises from the sea at the very moment the rose is born.

Gallica roses are also tough and survive in poor soil, but having been cultivated in ancient Greece and Rome they now respond to fertile ground and a place in the sun. A dense mass of harmless bristles and a few thorns which break off easily distinguish their stems; one is tempted to say they are a pleasure to handle. As old roses go, they are rather small shrubs with dark green leathery leaves and stalks holding their blooms aloft.

The flowers look very double, with lots of petals ranging in colour from shades of pink to exotic hues of crimson, purple and maroon. Their scent is often like that of white hyacinths.

Gallicas will flower without pruning. They can be improved, however, by the removal of one third of the new long stems after the old ones have flowered and been lightly cut. If grown as a low hedge, Gallica roses should be clipped with hand-shears in winter. Although they have a tendency to sucker, Gallicas are entirely suitable for the average size garden. For centuries *Rosa gallica* var. *officinalis*, the Apothecary's Rose, has been the rose most favoured for the scent of its dried petals. Another of Botticelli's paintings, *La Primavera*, includes what appear to be semi-double dark red Gallica roses.

Damask roses are close allies of Gallicas. They can usually be distinguished by their hips, which are elongated rather than round, and the downy appearance of their grey-green leaves. Borne in long clusters on the plant, the flowers are double, loose-petalled, in hues of pink and white, and of renowned fragrance. This fine scent is not 'free on the air' but close in the flower; it is from the Damask rose 'Professeur Emile Perrot' ('Kazanlik', see p.72) that rose oil is extracted for herbal remedies. The most well-known varieties in the garden are the striped York and Lancaster rose and the long-flowering 'Ispahan'. Damasks require no hard pruning and can simply be trimmed to shape.

For a long time Centifolia roses have been unflatteringly referred to as cabbage roses. This has nothing to do with their smell, which is heavenly, but the compaction of their petals. In the garden they can be lanky and disliked for their thorns but are redeemed by their exquisite flowers. 'A hundred petals' is an approximation, when the buds open the many petals move outward then reflex around the perimeter of the flower to reveal a

'Leda': An early nineteenth-century Gallica rose, renowned for fragrance and crimson markings on the rims of its outer petals, hence a more common name, the 'Painted Damask'. The otherwise milky blush flowers are double, with a button-eye centre.

'Henri Martin': A once-flowering Moss rose. The profusion of semi-double and clear crimson flower-clusters come through rainy weather relatively unscathed.

quartered formation with a green button eye at the centre. Intensely fragrant, Centifolias were at one time extensively grown for the manufacture of French perfume, but their oil has proved to be of a lower quality than that of Damask roses. Centifolia varieties range in colour from shades of clear and rose pink to cerise, purple and magenta. It is these roses which appear in many of the masterpieces of the Dutch flower-painters of the seventeenth and early eighteenth centuries, notably the *Vase with Flowers* by Jan van Huysum.

An interesting sub-group of Centifolias is that of Moss roses. They are distinguished by their resin-scented hairs, or bristles, which cover the flower-stalk and calyx. Some of this group can be encouraged to repeat their flowers by dead-heading. In winter the stems of all Centifolia roses should be reduced by one-third to one-half of their length.

The development of roses as plants for gardens and floristry was revolutionised when the first China roses arrived in Europe in the late eighteenth century. Their propensity to flower over a longer period at first made them objects of mere curiosity, their flowers were not particularly spectacular and somewhat lacking in fragrance. When crossed with European roses, however, the resulting hybrids sometimes combined the best qualities of both parents, thereby opening a new chapter in the history of cultivated roses, in which Hybrid Perpetual roses were the dominant class.

Many Hybrid Perpetual roses do not take their ability to repeat-flower from the China roses directly, but in combination with other smaller classes affected by the China introductions in varying degrees. Just to confuse matters, there was already one class in existence which had some ability to repeat its flowers despite the lack of a Far Eastern ancestor. An ancient silky-looking Damask rose, *R. damascena* var. *semperflorens* 'Quatre

Saisons', as its name implies, is remontant. Combined with the Apothecary's Rose, the resulting hybrid was cultivated on the estate of the Duchess of Portland in the eighteenth century. It was used to breed a class of valuable garden roses known as Portland roses.

At the beginning of the nineteenth century, cross-fertilisation between the same 'Quatre Saisons' and the Chinese rose 'Old Blush' (*R. X odorata* 'Pallida') occurred on the Ile de Bourbon, now called Réunion, in the southern Indian Ocean, where roses are commonly grown as hedges. In France, Antoine Jacques, head gardener to the Duc d'Orléans, received some of the resultant seedlings from the island's small botanic gardens. He was quick to recognise them as a valuable new class of repeat-flowering roses. They subsequently became known as Bourbons, which in the right conditions make good climbing roses.

China, Portland and Bourbon roses all played their part in the development of Hybrid Perpetuals, which range from short upright bushes to tall, lax shrubs, and can be adapted for use on walls, pillars and trellises. All of this second generation of old roses require rich soil, the pruning of their flowers by at least a third at the end of each season, and constant vigilance to guard against pests and diseases.

As the story of rose cultivation moves forward in time, the definition of what constitutes an old rose becomes ever more elusive. Certainly we need to include the scented Noisette roses, and ought not to omit Rugosa roses, which originated in Japan and are now widely used for hedges. Ramblers also divide into groups of their own which include wild species. Some of the varieties, like 'Rambling Rector' (*see* p.74), have obscure origins and are undoubtedly ancient. Others, including the most useful for growing on arches and pergolas, were hybridised by plantsmen using wild roses from Eastern China and Japan. Finally, we might add a small class of Hybrid Musk roses, bred in the years between the First and Second World Wars to be highly fragrant and just the right size for small gardens.

Most roses prefer to grow in direct sunlight, a few will tolerate shade, and all roses like to have their roots in cool moist ground. Similarly, all benefit from the enrichment of their soil, although Alba and Rambler roses suffer least from a loss of nourishment when adjacent to trees and other plants. Planting in ground that is rich in lime content or subject to water-logging is seldom successful. Of the herbalist John Gerarde (1545–1612) who made his garden in the fashionable London suburb of Holborn, it is said that he 'laboured with the soile to make it fit for plants, and with the plants, that they might delight in the soile'. Boasting of his old roses, Gerarde writes:

> These floure from the end of May to the end of August,
> the divers times after, by reason of the tops and superfluous
> branches are cut away in the end of their flouring: and then doe they
> sometimes floure even until October and after.

Growing roses separately from other plants is only an innovation of the last two hundred years. We might not be surprised that the Apothecary's Rose looks well among herbs, but the same could be said of nearly all the old shrub roses. The Portland rose 'Comte de Chambord' (see p.42) combines admirably with pots of herbs and has the advantage of flowering from early summer until the frosts set in. In *The Education of the Gardener* (1962), Russell Page describes his learning of 'how much body rose bushes will give to an herbaceous planting'. He imagined seeing 'amongst the bush roses, thick clumps of perennials … herbaceous paeonies and thalictrums and a dozen varieties of *Phlox paniculata* for their fresh colours and the honey sweetness they bring in late summer and all the Japanese anemones I could lay hands on'. In the Culpepper Garden at Leeds Castle

in Kent he realised a dream; bounded by clipped box hedges and columnar Irish yews, the bush roses are blended with bergamot, catmint, hardy geraniums, lupins and delphiniums.

Old roses are finding a place in gardens of all shapes and sizes. Without much restriction of their natural form they dwell happily among swaths of white foxgloves or scramble through trelliswork with *Clematis viticella* hard on their heels. Old roses have history attached to them to a degree unequalled by any other race of plants; among the 'dearest freshness deep down things', they are plants of incomparable beauty and deepest mystery.

Old roses associate well with racemes or spires of other flowers, plants such as lavender and foxgloves. At Nymans Garden, West Sussex, the Ramblers break into flower above mounds of the soft spikes of catmint.

class: **Rambler Sempervirens**
date: **1826**
grower: **Jacques**
flower: **semi-double**
colour: **white flushed pink**
scent: **primrose**
height: **5 metres**

Adélaide d'Orléans

'Adélaide d'Orléans' is a *Rosa sempervirens* hybrid and, in all but the severest of winters, always in leaf. It is elegant in growth and the full flowers come out in midsummer, pink in bud, blush white and semi-double on opening; they hang in loose clusters similar to the blossom on a cherry tree. Their scent is like that of primroses. This is a rose to train onto pillars, screens, archways and pergolas, wherever the flowers can captivate the senses at eye level: its ultimate height is 5 metres.

Antoine Jacques, head gardener to the Duc d'Orléans, claimed that the cross-pollination which produced his best roses was accidental. He seems to have had remarkable luck. The genetic fingerprint of the rose Adélaide d'Orléans shows it to be the result of crossing the wild evergreen rose of the Mediterranean region with the exotic 'Old Blush', the Chinese rose 'Yue Yue Fen', depicted in thousand-year-old paintings on silk. This rose reached Paris indirectly from Canton before 1798, and by the 1820s was widely distributed.

The real Princess Adélaide was tutored, along with her three brothers, in classics, modern languages and practical skills, including gardening. The children used their parents' estate as their huge playground, shocking honoured guests by diving headlong into the lake; considered to be quite eccentric in polite society. During the Revolution the entire family was put under sentence of death and, for reasons of security, the Princess went into exile for fourteen years, separated from her parents and siblings. They were reunited on the restoration of the monarchy. When her brother, Louis-Phillipe, was crowned King of France in 1830, Princess Adélaide became his most trusted adviser. The Princess's former home, the Hôtel Matignon, along with its huge garden, is today the official residence of the French Prime Minister.

In 1827, the year following his homage to the Princess, Jacques introduced 'Félicité Perpétue', a rose similar but more tolerant of a northerly aspect and with flowers fully double. Both this rose and 'Adélaide d'Orléans' should be compared with another lovely Rambler of more trailing habit, introduced by Albéric Barbier in 1900 and which bears his name.

class: **Wichuraiana Rambler**

date: **1909**

grower: **Barbier**

flower: **very double**

colour: **mauve to carmine**

scent: **apple**

height: **3.5 metres**

Alexandre Girault

The story of Wichuraiana Ramblers has its beginning with the Memorial Rose, which can be seen today in cemeteries throughout the USA, having been planted during the twentieth century. Forming a mass of glossy-dark and evergreen foliage, this useful ground cover is festooned in July with small white, clover-scented flowers, on whose mahogany-red hips the birds have their harvest supper.

In 1861 the botanist Max Ernst Wichura spotted such roses in the wild, trailing down rocks beside a river in Japan – the locals call it 'Teri-ha-no-ibara'. He shipped several of these plants to Europe but none survived the voyage. Dr Wichura was fated never again to set foot in Asia to repeat the process, he died shortly after his return to Germany.

Wichura's record of the rose, however, alerted other collectors and by 1880 botanical gardens in Munich and Brussels had procured living specimens. François Crépin, who was the Director at Brussels and who later advised Jules Gravereaux, the founder of La Roseraie de l'Haÿ in Paris, named it *Rosa wichuraiana* (now *Rosa wichurana*) to honour the memory of its discoverer. It is now commonly called the Memorial Rose.

Once *R. wichurana* was transported to North America, Michael Horvath, a nursery-hand on Rhode Island, cross-pollinated it to produce some interesting cultivars. His efforts attracted the attention of several rose-breeders who then extended his work, fashioning an entirely new range of Ramblers, the most popular of which is 'Dorothy Perkins' (1902).

Albéric Barbier also sent a plantsman to view Horvath's trials-fields and then used *R. wichurana* at his nursery in Orléans, France. The Barbier hybrids are especially graceful and grow like mantles over ground features; their fragrance is 'free on the air'. The most famous of these is 'Albertine' (1921) and among the most beautiful is 'Alexandre Girault', *R. wichurana* crossed with a pink Tea Rose to produce a soft, mauve flower; the petals slightly quilled, with a scent of sweet fresh apples.

Purists may regard 'Alexandre Girault' as modern, but it has pride of place in the dome at l'Haÿ, its distinctly old rose colour making it a feature in the world's greatest archive of the rose. In 1980 burglars broke into the pavilion of l'Haÿ and took scores of documents, some of which may have told us about the original Girault, one of Barbier's employees.

'Albertine': A 5-metre long Wichuraiana Rambler with large, very fragrant and loosely double flowers, lobster-pink, and gold at the base. The glossy foliage hides 'spiteful' thorns.

class: **Rambler**

date: **1824**

grower: **originated in China**

flower: **very double**

colour: **pale yellow/cream**

scent: **violets**

height: **6 metres**

Banksiae Lutea

Banksian roses are named in honour of Lady Dorothea Banks, the wife of the renowned botanist, Sir Joseph Banks. These plants are vigorous ramblers, producing flexible, green almost thornless canes about 6 metres in length. Because the flowers are borne in trusses on side-shoots, most profusely when these are two or three years old, pruning involves removing any very old wood and some of the five-year-old canes, leaving the remainder to flower another two or three years. *Rosa banksiae lutea* is the hardiest variety and flowers best on a sheltered south-facing wall; although only slightly fragrant, it is one of the world's finest roses, with 'large hanging sprays of tiny, double, pale yellow flowers'.

Sir Joseph Banks (1743–1820) was heir to a fortune, which allowed him to spend his life in enthusiastic pursuit of plants from all corners of the earth. He explored the wild coastland of Newfoundland and voyaged around the world aboard the *Endeavour* with Captain Cook. For 41 years he was President of the Royal Society, where he acquired a reputation as 'a benevolent scientific despot'. During this period, he continued plant-hunting by proxy. In 1803, it was Banks who arranged for a Kew gardener, William Kerr, to become the first professional plant-collector in the Far East.

On his arrival in China, Kerr found no favour with a government determined to keep prying foreigners out of the interior. Just three days a month he was permitted to visit the Fa-tee, or 'Flowery Land', an island nursery up-river from Canton. Inadequately paid, it is a miracle he survived in the post for nine years, sending back to England a fine haul of plants and bulbs, among them: *Kerria japonica*, named after himself; tiger lilies, which were successfully propogated; and the violet-scented *Rosa banksiae alba plena*. William Kerr did eventually leave China to superintend the Ceylon Botanical Garden in Columbo, where he died in 1814 of 'some illness incidental to the climate'.

Rosa banksiae lutea was brought to England ten years later by John Damper Parks. On behalf of the Horticultural Society of London, he set out for China in 1823 and returned in May of the following year with this rose, new cultivars of chrysanthemums and camellias, and 'Parks' Yellow Tea-scented China' rose. This last proved vital for the breeding of our modern roses.

class: **Multiflora Rambler**

date: *c.* **1900**

grower: **unknown**

flower: **double**

colour: **violet crimson**

scent: **grassy/floral**

height: **4–5 metres**

Bleu Magenta

No one has done more than Graham Stuart Thomas to raise a serious appreciation of old roses, having written several books about them explaining their characteristics and others citing their use in garden design. He was quick to correct a comment about the colour blue in roses during a visit to his home and garden one fine July morning in 2002. There is no blue flower in roses, apparently; even the modern rose 'Blue Moon' is commonly described as a mixture of lilac and mauve, too metallic for some tastes. The accurate description for what we call dark blue or grape purple is 'murrey', a word derived from the Latin description of the inimitable colour of dark mulberries.

The small group of old roses with flowers that tend towards murrey share the disadvantage of having not much fragrance, with the exception of 'Veilchenblau', which has a lovely scent of citrus fruit. This rose has always been listed in good nursery catalogues, whilst 'Bleu Magenta' is seldom found. Graham Stuart Thomas brought some 'Bleu Magenta' into England from the immense collection of cultivars at the Roseraie de l'Haÿ near Paris. He has planted these Ramblers in a circle of arches in the triangular part of the walled rose garden at Mottisfont Abbey, Hampshire. Described as a pillar rose, though best not planted too near the dry ground of a wall, 'Bleu Magenta' grows almost thornless canes up to a length of 4 or 5 metres. The leaves are shining dark green and the double flowers are borne in clusters, the petals white at the base as if not fully dipped in a dye of dark violet crimson.

Even more than other garden roses, 'Bleu Magenta' needs to be planted in cool, rich and moisture-retentive soil if it is not to suffer mildew; it blossoms later in the summer than most old roses, when the ground is in danger of being dry. The colour of this rose, however one dares to describe it, goes well with any flower that is rose pink. At Mottisfont (*opposite*) it is displayed to marvellous effect in the company of the rose 'Débutante'.

class: **Hybrid Musk**
date: **1939**
grower: **Bentall**
flower: **double**
colour: **apricot/yellow**
scent: **tea/violets/banana**
height: **1.5 metres**

Buff Beauty

Learning about old roses inevitably leads to a consideration of the merits of the new roses, those especially bred for their old-fashioned characteristics. The leading rose-grower in this respect is David Austin, whose nursery at Albrighton has a well laid-out and wonderfully peaceful old rose garden. Long aisles lead the visitor through beds of Gallicas, Albas, Centifolias and Damasks, and at the junction of the pathways are pergolas bearing the different Climbers and Ramblers. Michael Marriott, the head of the nursery's advisory staff, suggested the inclusion in any collection of the old roses, of at least one or two Hybrid Musks, fore-runners of his nursery's English Roses.

'Buff Beauty' is a Hybrid Musk and the youngest rose to be featured in this book. Its large and fully double flowers are borne in small clusters in summer and again in long panicles on new shoots towards autumn. According to soil conditions and the weather, the colour of the flowers varies, from apricot to primrose, the scent is always strong and delicious, a mixture of tea, violets and unripe banana. The branches are graceful and arching, bearing dark green leaves, somewhat bronze on the new growth. As a border shrub or container plant this rose grows to 1.5 metres. If grown on a pillar or against a wall, the soil will need to be enriched to drive the rose higher. As with the others of its class, 'Buff Beauty' can be planted to make an attractive rose hedge. To encourage blooms of high quality, it is important to dead-head during the summer and shorten the canes by a third or more in winter, at the same time removing old and twiggy wood from the base.

The Hybrid Musk roses were raised by an exceedingly knowledgeable, amateur rose-grower, the Reverend Joseph Pemberton, an Anglican priest who lived in the old Round House at Havering-atte-Bower, Essex. He and his sister Florence also proved to be good tutors of horticulture, as it is to two of his gardeners, John and Ann Bentall, that we owe the introduction of 'Buff Beauty'. All of Pemberton's Hybrid Musks have distinctively healthy dark foliage, which offsets the light pastel shades of the different varieties. All of them normally have two flowering flushes and a lovely fragrance. In the *Rose Annual* of 1923, Pemberton wrote: 'The time is coming when a distinct class, termed Shrub Roses, will obtain official recognition'. This is the prophecy that David Austin has sought to bring to fruition.

class: **Gallica**

date: **1840**

grower: **Laffay**

flower: **very double**

colour: **velvet purple**

scent: **floral/peppery**

height: **1–1.5 metres**

Cardinal de Richelieu

Although the Gallicas are probably the oldest class of cultivated roses, the ancient Mediterranean civilisations seem not to have had a rose as deep in colour as 'Cardinal de Richelieu'. The flowers are very double, velvet-dusky purple when fully open. As they emerge from the round bud the petals appear almost pink, the outermost then peeling away from the dome and growing darker. When all have reflexed, the flower is a peony-like ball of rolled petals the colour of dark mulberries, smelling of Turkish Delight and somewhat peppery. The colour of the petals towards the centre is whitened a little, near to where there is an apple-green eye to the flower.

'Maiden's Blush': Slightly smaller (1.2m) in size and flower to 'Great Maiden's Blush' (1.8m), but in all other respects the same medieval Alba rose, known in France by several names: 'Cuisse de Nymphe', 'Incarnata', 'La Virginale' and 'La Seduisante'. It has wonderful blush-pink, double flowers, muddled at the centre and sweetly scented.

'Cardinal de Richelieu' is an ideal pillar rose, strong but not too vigorous. In a patio container it can be maintained at a height of one metre. If it is grown higher in the flower border Graham Stuart Thomas suggests planting it next to one or more of the light Albas, 'Celeste' and 'Great Maiden's Blush'. The stems have few thorns and the leaves are a smooth dark green. The Staffordshire nurseryman John Scarman recommends placing 'Richelieu' next to grey-leaved plants and in particular the rose pink-flowered verbascum.

Gallica roses regained favour in Western Europe once the Church had largely forgotten their association with pagan Rome, and they reappeared in religious art in the fifteenth century. However, the naming of this rose after a renowned Church prelate more was to do with recognition of his political astuteness than his piety. Richelieu was a shrewd but ruthless operator, and the effective ruler of France on behalf of King Louis XIII. In 1628 he starved the Huguenot nobles into submission at La Rochelle and then weakened the power of rival European states by a combination of war and intrigue. His influence on the cultural life of France was lasting – he founded the *Jardin des Plantes* in Paris and the French Academy.

class: **Damask**
date: **prior to 1732**
grower: **unknown**
flower: **semi-double**
colour: **warm light pink**
scent: **lemon/almonds**
height: **1.5 metres**

Celsiana

This flower was held in high regard by the Dutch horticulturists of the eighteenth century and appears to be one of the roses in the flower paintings of the artists Jan van Huysum and Rachel Rusch. The flowers are semi-double, light pink, petals silk-like and ruffled, not quite hiding the yellow stamens, the strong scent is that of lemon zest with almonds. In sunlight the flowers fade to blush pink but lose none of their beauty. The changes in colour during flowering gave to 'Celsiana' a variety of names: 'Rose Varin', 'La Coquette', 'Damascena Mutabilis'. It had been imported from Holland into France by the plant breeder Jacques-Martin Cels. On Cels' death, this rose was the means by which he came to be remembered, the other names falling into disuse.

'Celsiana' has all the attributes of the Damask roses, not least a strong and complex fragrance the character of which can only be hinted at by allusion to other natural scents. According to legend, the crusader Robert de Brie was the first to bring these roses from Damascus to France, to his castle in Champagne in the thirteenth century. They arrived in England much later, during the reign of Henry VIII, transported from Italy by his physician Thomas Linacre, the founder of the Royal College of Physicians.

There are now two forms of the Damask rose, both of them having been derived from cross-breeding with the highly fragrant Apothecary's Rose. The first are the summer-flowering Damasks, which come from an association with *Rosa phoenicia*, the wild Rambler rose of Turkey and Syria. The second type are the repeat-flowering Autumn Damasks, hybrids from association with *Rosa moschata*, the Mediterranean Musk Rose. All Damask roses are distinguished by their long, pointed greyish-green leaves, downy on the underside, on shrubs of between 1 and 2 metres high. Their flower colours range from white to clear pink and the flowers are carried on frail stalks in long airy sprays. 'Celsiana' is ideal for a shrub border, when not in flower its foliage offsets the flowers of other plants perfectly.

class: **Centifolia**
date: **1826**
grower: **Vibert**
flower: **very double**
colour: **deep pink**
scent: **sweet/peppery**
height: **1.5 metres**

Chapeau de Napoléon

No other rose is as unusual and beautiful in the bud as *R. X centifolia* 'Cristata' or 'Chapeau de Napoléon'. The calyx, which consists of the sepals enclosing the tightly-packed flower before its opening, carry a unique fern-like crest. Hence it is sometimes called 'Crested Moss', although on a true moss rose these whiskers would cover the entire calyx and the flower-stalk. Before the bud bursts, revealing the deep pink petals of the double flower, the shape of the bearded calyx resembles a cocked hat of the type worn by Napoleon. The scent of the flower is powerfully sweet and peppery. 'Chapeau de Napoléon' grows up to 1.5 metres with attractive foliage, making it a very acceptable shrub in a mixed border and a good source of blooms for flower arrangements.

Plants often grow on ruined walls. The most successful in this respect are ferns and buddleias which seem to enjoy rooting in old mortar almost as much as in good soil. Similarly in 1820, the rose destined for fame as 'Chapeau de Napoléon' was discovered by chance rooted on the top of an old tower at a nunnery in Fribourg, Switzerland. The plant seems to have grown from the seed of a Centifolia garden rose which had been dropped into the crevice by a careless bird. What caused it to hybridise into such an exotic flower-bud we shall never know. However, once it had been taken into France and became the property of the nursery of Vibert in Angers, its place in the portfolio of the world's most interesting roses was assured.

As for Napoleon himself, we can commend him for the freedom he gave Josephine (see 'Empress Josephine', p.48) to indulge her obsession with roses, even if he sometimes griped at the cost, and occasionally took a dislike to her plantsmen. He sacked one of them for having moved a shrub without authorisation. After an indecently short interlude Josephine reinstated the man. The gardener in question was Charles Mirbel, for whom she endowed a professorship at the Sorbonne. In this refuge he felt sufficiently far removed from the Emperor's displeasure to settle down and write several books on horticulture.

class: **Gallica**

date: **1790**

grower: **François**

flower: **very double**

colour: **crimson/purple**

scent: **floral/resinous**

height: **1.25 metres**

Charles de Mills

Rose experts of recent times have regarded 'Charles de Mills' as something of an enigma. Jack Harkness found no mention of this cultivar in nineteenth-century English catalogues and conjectured it was not old. Peter Beales lists 'Charles de Mills' as having a strong scent and says that he can find no convincing explanation of its naming. Graham Stuart Thomas also has no circumstantial history to offer but is impressed by the flower 'resembling an African marigold but with much more quality', unfortunately with 'little fragrance'.

To these contrasting assessments of fragrance we can add the view of the Elizabethan philosopher and statesman, Sir Francis Bacon. He observed that 'roses damask and red [i.e., Gallica] are fast flowers of their smells'. In other words, the petals are retentive of scented oil, which of course makes them ideal for pot-pourri, and for flavouring wines, preserves and confectionery. 'Charles de Mills' has a deeply floral and resinous fragrance, akin to retsina wine.

The shrub is compact, 1.25 metres, and almost thornless. The flower is exceptional: out of a bud which looks as if it had been sliced horizontally emerges a full and perfectly formed cup of crimson petals. When fully open, this flower quarters and varies in colour from crimson-purple to dark lilac, with a green eye at its centre. So intense are the crimson tones that in the half-light of evening the flower is luminous.

Such a rose would certainly have been prized in eighteenth-century Holland, where it was once thought to have originated. In France it was called 'Bizarre Triomphant' and, having been introduced by François in 1790, appeared thirteen years later in the catalogue of J.L. Descemet, who supplied part of the rose collection of the Empress Josephine. Not surprisingly, in view of this provenance, it appears in Vibert's catalogues of the 1820s (see ' Petite Lisette', p.70).

The rose gained its current name in the 1830s, when there was indeed a nurseryman called Charles Mills at Blyth in Nottinghamshire. A more romantic origin for the name is suggested by a Monsieur Louiseleur-Deslongchamps who, in 1844, recalled an Englishman in Rome by the name of Mills, famous for his '*pergola Italiénne, tapisée des roses Bengale*' – a colourful display of China roses imported from India.

class: **unclassified**
date: **indeterminate**
grower: **unknown**
flower: **single**
colour: **bright pink**
scent: **sweet/musk**
height: **up to 3 metres**

Complicata

This flower is spectacular and, in colour at least, is not what we might expect of an old rose. The single blooms are a bright, almost shocking pink and at least 10cm across. The petals pale towards the centre of the flower, giving its honey-yellow stamens a soft halo. The scent from the stamens is musk, from the petals typically that of a Gallica rose, overall it is sweet and hinting of a fine cigar.

Graham Stuart Thomas grows this rose on poor soil in his garden where it sprawls 3 metres up into an apple tree. 'It should be in every garden where shrubs are grown', he writes, 'in full flower no shrub is more spectacular'. The flowers are borne in long sprays on the arching branches which, if unsupported, will grow just short of 2 metres. Tolerant of partial shade, it is a good shrub for woodland. Another of its uses is to make a tall hedge: the leaves are large, mid-green and profuse.

One of the nineteenth century's great scientists, Jean Grenier, observed that a certain wild rose only grew in the tree line of the French Alps near to where he lived, at 800 to 1,000 metres. He noted its single pink flowers followed by deep orange wax hips and, for reasons we may never know, called it 'Complicata'. In 1902 Jules Gravereaux, having made a fortune pioneering the Bon Marché, the world's first department store, ordered a specimen of Grenier's wild alpine rose for his new public garden in the Paris suburb of l'Haÿ, where he was planning to display every variety of rose in the world.

However, the rose Gravereaux received was not the rose he ordered. The Otto Froebel nursery at Zurich inadvertently sent an accidental hybrid: the correct wild rose crossed with a Gallica. Gallica roses seldom venture up mountains.

Nobody suspected anything amiss and for the next 23 years visitors to l'Haÿ admired 'Complicata' and bought it for their gardens. When the authenticity of this rose was finally questioned, the popularity of the crossed 'Complicata' had ruled out any hope of correcting the error. The real 'Complicata', which almost slipped back into anonymity among the fir trees, is now called *Rosa glauca* Pourr.

class: **Portland**

date: **1863**

grower: **Moreau-Robert**

flower: **very double**

colour: **pink/lilac**

scent: **sweet and spicy**

height: **1.5 metres**

Comte de Chambord

'Jacques Cartier': A light, clear pink Portland rose introduced by the nursery of Moreau-Robert in 1868. The scented flowers are fully double, quartered, with a pronounced button-eye; flatter, less cupped and more ragged than 'Comte de Chambord', but hardly less beautiful. Portland Roses are ideal for growing in containers.

The DIY megastore is not normally the first port of call when purchasing an old rose. My curiosity was aroused in the gardening department when I spotted a trolley-load of very healthy and distinctly bushy-looking roses with plenty of lush green foliage. On closer inspection they turned out to be 'Jacques Cartier', named after the explorer of the St Lawrence, just the right cultivar for the first time buyer. There is only one other old rose in the Portland class I would rate higher, and that is 'Comte de Chambord'.

The Portland roses are a small class positioned between the Gallicas and the Damasks, having started up when the Apothecary's Rose crossed with 'Quatre Saisons', the latter providing the power of repeat-flowering, or remontancy. 'Comte de Chambord' is one of the earliest to bloom and goes on in splendour until the first frosts. The strongly fragrant flowers are large, sometimes quartered, rich pink with a hint of lilac, and dense with rolled petals, reflexed at the outer edges. The Staffordshire horticulturist John Scarman records this rose as first raised in America, and called 'Madame Boll' before its introduction in France by Moreau-Robert at Angers.

The original Comte de Chambord was heir to the French throne and suffered the misfortune of having a father who was assassinated before he was born. He grew up at a time of political disorder and for security clung to the traditions of a bygone age. In the revolution of 1830 his grandfather abdicated in his favour when he was only ten, having indoctrinated him in the divine right of kings. However, he had to give way to the Duc d'Orléans who became the Citizen King, Louis-Phillipe. Known as Henry V to his supporters, the Comte de Chambord disdained the tricolour in favour of the white flag of the Old Kings, but he lost any further chance of the throne. History has not been kind to him and he has been condemned as weak and indecisive as well as reactionary. He died in Austria in 1883 without issue. Perhaps his greatest memorial was to give his title to this rose.

class: **Noisette**
date: **1826**
grower: **Desprez**
flower: **double**
colour: **apricot/peach**
scent: **pineapple/hyacinth**
height: **5 metres**

Desprez à Fleur Jaunes

The Noisette roses originated in America around 1800 and they are generally accredited to the work of a Charleston nurseryman, Philippe Noisette. The horticulturists of Rouen, however, claim that a rose-grower on Long Island was the first to cross the China rose, 'Old Blush', with a Musk rose. Whoever was first, the result of this crossbreeding was a hybrid, which Philippe Noisette named after a wealthy rice-planter, John Champneys, a patron of his nursery. 'Champneys Pink Cluster' is the first truly repeat-flowering cultivar to have been bred in the western hemisphere, it is the rose from which this class, including a rose called 'Blush Noisette', is derived. These roses are all deliciously fragrant and grow well on walls, pergolas and arches in sheltered, warm locations.

'Desprez à Fleur Jaunes' is the result of crossing 'Blush Noisette' with a yellow Tea Rose. To encourage its flowering, 'Desprez à Fleur Jaunes' needs to be planted against a protected south-facing wall. The flowers when they open are silk-like, creamy with colours of peach, apricot and yellow. A French newspaper at the time this rose was first exhibited described the scent as 'a heady mix of tea, pineapple and hyacinth'. In England a *Manual of Roses* in 1846 declared that, 'one plant will perfume a large garden in the cool weather of autumn'.

'Desprez à Fleur Jaunes' came from the same garden in the village of Yèbles as 'Baronne Prévost' and 'Général Soyez', legendary roses bred by the retired civil servant Jean Desprez. He refused to let others grow his roses until a 3000-franc bill for a new greenhouse goaded him to sell the rights to a Dutch horticulturist Sysley-Vandaël. On the same day Sysley-Vandaël launched 'Desprez à Fleur Jaunes' at his new nursery in Paris, other nurseries began selling an identical variety at half the price. Someone had stolen cuttings! Sysley-Vandaël began a criminal investigation only to find himself successfully sued by the French growers for defamation.

Other Noisette climbing roses, hardy and fragrant, are 'Aimée Vibert' and 'Madam Alfred Carrière'. The second of these is much more vigorous and will grow on a north-facing wall while still providing marvellous blooms for indoor displays.

Eglantine

Set on plinths around the Victorian Palm House of Sefton Park in Liverpool are statues of great explorers, botanists and gardeners, monuments from a period when the city was one of the world's great sea-ports. The garden designer André le Nôtre and the apothecary John Parkinson stand on opposite sides of the main entrance, and on the west side stands Linnaeus dressed in the native costume of Lapland, the country in which he made an extensive survey of the wild plants.

Linnaeus' two great contributions to the advancement of science were to classify plants according to their sexual characteristics and to identify each of them by the ascription of two Latin words, a generic name followed by a specific epithet. Hence the Eglantine was called *Rosa eglanteria* (now *R. rubiginosa*). There is another more common name for the Eglantine on account of a delicious apple fragrance released from its leaf-glands when they have been touched by a moist westerly wind or bruised by the rain; the rose is sometimes called the Sweet Briar.

Had Linnaeus been mindful of this delightful common name he might not have committed an appalling gaffe. He inadvertently gave the Latin name of the Eglantine to the evil-smelling Austrian Yellow Briar, leaving the Sweet Briar with the title *Rosa rubiginosa*, the rust rose, so called after its supposedly red foliage! The Austrian Yellow was eventually quite rightly called *Rosa foetida*, the rose that stinks.

The 3-metre long and well-armed stems of the Eglantine make it ideal for a country-mixture hedgerow (see 'Rosa Canina', p.76), or spaced at 1-metre intervals this briar alone can make a hedge up to 2 metres wide. For a combination of arching stems, fine fragrance and delicacy of flower, no other wild rose matches it.

For some reason the birds eat the hips of Dog Roses and leave those of the Eglantine alone. These hips are used to manufacture rose-hip seed oil which, if gently rubbed on scar tissue or damaged skin, prevents blistering. The hip oil unfortunately does not have the sweet scent of the Eglantine's leaves.

class: **Gallica**
date: **prior to 1820**
grower: **unknown**
flower: **double**
colour: **deep pink**
scent: **spice/vanilla**
height: **1.2 metres**

Empress Josephine

This is a lovely flower with loose, deep pink veined petals and a most delicate perfume. Its origin is uncertain, a rose similar in almost every detail was recorded by the botanist Clusius (the Latinised name of Charles de l'Ecluse) in the sixteenth century. Ideal for setting alongside other shrubs and herbs, this rose can be planted in a border or in a pot, and like all Gallicas it is a strong grower. The Empress of France, as far as we know, did not wish her name to be used on a specific variety during her lifetime, but this posthumous title has great historic resonance.

The Empress Josephine was Marie-Joseph-Rose, the most beautiful daughter of an impoverished aristocrat, who was married at fourteen to the Vicomte de Beauharnais. They lived on Martinique and had two sons when, in spite of Beauharnais' loyal service to the Revolution, they fell under suspicion. Josephine narrowly escaped with her life, but her husband was sent to the guillotine in 1794.

Two years after this tragedy she met and married Napoleon Bonaparte, who had fallen deeply in love with her. When Napoleon became Emperor their home at La Malmaison near Paris gained a reputation throughout Europe as a centre of culture and gaiety. Josephine restored the Château, which had been used as a sanatorium, and with her designer Jean Marie Morel created an enchanting garden. It contained a stream, a lake, a temple, a hothouse and a salon with plant-entwined marble pillars and settees. From her sofa next to the miniature waterfall built of artificial rock, the Empress regaled her guests with the Latin names of some 200 varieties of plants she had imported, regardless of naval blockades, from all corners of the world.

Josephine collected over two hundred rose cultivars, intending to send progeny for the planting of rosaries in every Department of France. She commissioned the Ardennes artist Pierre-Joseph Redouté to produce hundreds of paintings of many of her plants, including the 169 which appeared after her death in the first edition of *Les Roses*. She and Napoleon had no children and divorced in 1809. Josephine died in 1814, having played a crucial role in the development of rose horticulture.

class: **Centifolia**
date: *c.* **1900**
grower: **unknown**
flower: **very double**
colour: **shell pink**
scent: **citrus**
height: **1.5–3 metres**

Fantin-Latour

There is often some mystery about the origin of particular varieties of old roses but few are as conspicuously lacking any record as 'Fantin-Latour'. There is no mention of this rose before the nineteenth century and no hint as to its identification under any other name. This is made all the more intriguing by the fact that this rose has possibly the best flower of any of the Centifolias, bursting waves of blush pink petals, deepening to shell pink at the centre, the outer petals reflexed. Centifolia roses are noted for the intensity of their fragrance but the perfume of this rose, though strong, is somewhat lighter, similar to that of Alba roses and with a dominant note of citrus.

Tolerant of poor soils, 'Fantin-Latour' can be left to grow into a rounded shrub 1.5 metres in height, or grown against a wall, it will reach 3 metres or more. It requires thinning to keep it vigorous, removing the old wood. Due, it is thought, to the influence of a China rose somewhere in its genetic make-up, the leaves are more rounded and darker green than most Centifolias, which are generally grey-green in colour.

Henri Fantin-Latour (1836–1904), an outstanding painter of roses, joined the Salon des Refusés – which was the first gathering of the Impressionists – yet he is often described as conservative in both his work and his life. This is to ignore the vitality of his paintings in comparison with the vast output of botanical drawings of roses in this period. His work is impressionistic in the best sense of the word, the roses are often reflected on glass or polished wood and, in the words of one critic, 'are unsurpassed in their freedom and spontaneity'.

The mystery rose which became 'Fantin-Latour' could only have gained its name from the fact that it seemed to embody the rhythmic beauty of the flowers as this artist painted them.

Henri Fantin-Latour, *Roses in a Glass Vase*, 1876.

50

Frau Karl Druschki

In a sorry endeavour to cover up its Teutonic origin, in England the name of this rose was changed to 'Snow Queen' during the First World War. It has always had an enthusiastic following despite one drawback, best illustrated in a story told by the writer and rose-grower George Taylor in the 1927 *Rose Annual*:

> A very enthusiastic gardener asked me to name what I considered the best white Rose. It was in the days when 'Frau Karl Druschki' was supreme; it was all the rage, and no other variety was then supposed to rival the great 'Snow Queen'. I said so. "No", he replied, "I do not want 'Frau Karl Druschki'; that Rose always reminds me of a beautiful woman without a character". The reference, of course, applied to its lack of fragrance. Every rose should have a perfume, a fragrance peculiarly its own.

The explanation as to why a rose without scent continues to find a market lies in its large, pure white globular flowers, which can look so striking in situations where other, highly-perfumed plants might have less impact. These flowers look quite modern, but the shrub has all the appearance of an old variety.

'Frau Karl Druschki' is also a good rose for pegging down. This practice involves allowing the rose to grow naturally after having been hard pruned when planted. In the second year the stems are trained by means of wire pegs parallel to the ground, at a height of 30cm. The rose will then send up flowering shoots, which can be pruned and spurred, similar to those of a fruit tree, at the end of the flowering season. Eventually old and less productive stems can be removed in favour of the new more vigorous ones. In this way one rose will cover a wide area, provided weeds are controlled with the aid of bark mulching. Our Victorian ancestors usually grew their Hybrid Perpetuals in this way.

Peter Lambert of Trier entered his new rose in the Frankfurt Show of 1900. He anticipated a prize of 3,000 marks and the right to name it Otto von Bismarck. Failing to win he took some consolation in hearing the judges' cries of regret over their decision when they later toured his fields and saw how well it grew. In Berlin his rose finally swept the board and earned the name of the wife of the presiding judge. This lady was never, as far as I am aware, called the Snow Queen.

class: **Hybrid Perpetual**
date: **1853**
grower: **Roussel**
flower: **semi-double**
colour: **rich crimson**
scent: **floral/peppery**
height: **1.5 metres**

Général Jacqueminot

An amateur rose-grower of Montpelier, M.A. Roussel, raised seedling roses but found no good ones. Shortly after his death his gardener examined the last lot and found this rich crimson, highly fragrant rose among them. It was named after a war hero who had distinguished himself in the disastrous invasion of Russia in 1812. When Napoleon wanted a Russian to interrogate, Jacqueminot rode forth into a band of Cossacks, scooped up an officer whom he threw across his saddle and swam back with him across the icy River Berezina.

Affectionately known in Britain and America as 'General Jack', Roussel's rose with its fresh green foliage quickly became sought after as the most outstanding of the red roses with shapely pointed buds and well-formed fully double flowers on long stems. The 27 petals each have a white flash on the underside and their scent is Damask-like: floral, peppery and narcotic.

For all these reasons 'Général Jacqueminot' became a favourite of the rose shows and in demand for professional floristry. It was recommended for medicinal use in Mrs Grieve's *A Modern Herbal* (1931) and for a short time was grown for the extraction of rose oil. Only with the advent of Hybrid Tea roses was it ousted from the shrub border by flowers of a brighter colour. Like many Hybrid Perpetuals, the General is prone to fungal diseases requiring the gardener to spray the plant constantly and pile on the manure. It is particularly susceptible to deadly rust.

Trading on the enormous popularity of this rose, a perfume called 'La Rose Jacqueminot' was launched in 1904, the first of several created by François Coty who had trained as a fragrance assessor at Grasse. He knew the power of marketing and commissioned the Art Nouveau jewellery designer René Lalique to make prototypes for scent bottles. Having unsuccessfully touted 'La Rose Jacqueminot' around Paris, at his last and again unsuccessful port of call, the Louvre Department Store, Coty dropped and smashed a bottle of his perfume in the aisle on his way out. A flurry of excitement ensued from shoppers eager to know where they might buy the gorgeous fragrance. This caused the store's purchasing manager to change his mind, of course, and other stores followed suit. The perfume is no longer available but the rose, for all its faults, is in a few nursery catalogues, and will remain there on the merits of its colour, fragrance and the recommendation of its devotees.

Goldfinch

Multiflora means that the flowers are borne in clusters, the overall effect of which is breathtakingly lovely in the case of a rose like 'Goldfinch', one of the best among the 'thornless' roses. Each small cupped flower is semi-double, orange-yellow around the dark yellow stamens and primrose fading to white at the outer edges. The scent is unmistakably of fruit: oranges and bananas. In moderately hot sun these flowers fade quickly and become like little pieces of crushed pure white paper wrapped around the shoots.

After years of neglect, 'Goldfinch' is one of the roses most frequently rediscovered in old gardens, its green-brown stems and glossy foliage having blended unnoticed into some background wilderness. If planted new it can either be grown as a shrub or trailed over a tree-stump, a tripod or a hedge. For flower arrangements the stems need to be cut whilst in bud and the flowers allowed to open indoors, in that way they retain their colour. But beware the underside of the petioles, where there is one vicious barb.

The nurseryman George Paul, of Cheshunt in Hertfordshire, no doubt leapt with joy at having bred such a delightful yellow rambler as 'Goldfinch'. A none too vigorous climbing rose was the sort he knew his customers would be eager to plant in their gardens at the leafier extremes of North London. Unfortunately for him, the rose roots so easily from cuttings that most gardeners are able to obtain it for free from their friends. Paul gained little financial reward for having bred the friendliest of roses.

When choosing a thornless climbing rose, most people it seems still opt for 'Zéphirine Drouhin', a beautiful cerise-pink Bourbon, sweetly-scented and flowering late into autumn. This is to mention its good points. It is prone to mildew and in my experience making it work properly requires a lot of care and attention, specifically mulching and spraying.

'Zéphirine Drouhin', looking exceedingly healthy and reaching its maximum height of 3 metres. This popular rose was first marketed by a little-known nurseryman, Bizot, in 1868.

class: **Moss**
date: **1863**
grower: **Laffay**
flower: **semi-double**
colour: **clear crimson**
scent: **pepper/orange**
height: **1.5 metres**

Henri Martin

We now come to the phantoms of the opera, a curious, some would say grotesque, group of mutant roses that were highly fashionable in Victorian times. They are the Moss roses, freaked-out Centifolia roses with whiskers all over the flower stem and the calyx of the bud. These whiskers are gross protrusions of the plants' glands, they can be as stiff as bristles on some varieties or as soft as moss on others. If stroked, the whiskers impart to the hands a sharp resinous and balsamic odour.

Among the Moss roses, one of the most graceful is the 'Old Red Moss', now named 'Henri Martin' in honour of a renowned French historian. It has plentiful dark green foliage and clusters of bright crimson flowers, scented pepper and orange. The shrub grows to 1.5 metres and, provided the soil is moist, it can be grown against a north wall.

The first Moss Rose arrived in England in the eighteenth century, a variety known as 'Old Pink Moss' (*Rosa* X *centifolia* 'Muscosa') which is still prized for its fragrance. An accurate description of it appeared in the first-ever *Gardeners Dictionary* of 1760. The author of this important botanical reference work was Philip Miller, the first Curator of the Chelsea Physic Garden. A cantankerous man, he was dismissed from the post at the age of seventy-nine for 'obstinacy and impertinence'. The number of species brought under cultivation in Britain during Miller's lifetime soared from about 1,000 to 5,000, many of them introduced by Miller himself. The names and origin of these he kept secret, in case another horticulturist stole his show. He had a habit, however, of discarding the wrappers from his imports in the Thames. and one of his former pupils, the nurseryman James Lee, 'kept a boy for the express purpose of retrieving them even if he had to swim, and was thus informed of all the new acquisitions'.

The original Moss Rose described by Miller was not kept a secret but virtually ignored until it was taken up in France for breeding. Vibert produced the pink-flowered 'Zoé' in 1830 and in 1845 Laffay caused a sensation with 'Nuits de Young', known in England as 'Old Black Moss'. This astonishingly dark, velvety-maroon flower emboldened Laffay to announce that 'from the moss roses we shall soon see great things'. Over the next 40 years hundreds of Moss cultivars were marketed but not many fulfilled Laffay's expectations. The best have survived, and they are few, 'Henri Martin' happily among them.

class: **Alba**
date: **1826**
grower: **Booth**
flower: **very double**
colour: **soft pink**
scent: **lemon/sea spray**
height: **1.5 metres**

Königin von Dänemark

Few roses attract the sort of acclaim given to 'Königin von Dänemark'; it bears all the attributes anyone could wish for in an old rose. An intense soft pink, the double flowers open from a very compacted and somewhat flattened bud. The flower-cup as it expands retains the inward curvature of the enclosed petals; their colour grows lighter as the outermost petals reflex and those in the cup become quartered and chiffoné, with a button-eye at their centre. In her *Garden Book* (1968), Vita Sackville-West describes the flowers as 'looking as though someone has taken a spoon and stirred it round as a child might stir a bowl of strawberries and cream'. In the final stage of opening the petals relax and straighten.

The fragrance of this rose is gorgeous, reminiscent of sea air and lemons. Trained onto a small tree, the scented flower-heads hang down at eye-level from lovely dark blue-green and very elegant foliage. 'Königin von Dänemark' is a seedling of that other great rose of the Alba group, 'Great Maiden's Blush', with flowers which are somewhat lighter in colour.

After painstaking trials lasting ten years, James Booth & Söhne of Klein-Flottbeck near Altona in Southern Denmark entered their new rose in the catalogue of 1826. They were then attacked by the director of Hamburg Botanic Gardens, Professor Lehmann, who argued that the cultivar was not new but already well-known in France. There followed a vitriolic exchange of published letters, the upshot of which was that the Professor failed to prove his case and the rose was accredited to the nursery. The Booths had named it after Marie Sofie Frederikke of Hesse-Cassel, wife of King Frederick VI of Denmark. Despite the part he played in the currency dealing which helped bankrupt the economy of his kingdom, the King and his Queen were immensely popular. Sunday afternoons saw the royal couple being rowed on the canals of Copenhagen to the applause of their loyal subjects. The naming of the rose was an act of genuine affection, with an eye to success.

class: **China**
date: **1859**
grower: **Guillot Fils**
flower: **semi-double**
colour: **deep crimson**
scent: **earth/violets**
height: **0.6 metres**

Louis XIV

Few roses can approach the velvet crimson of this almost double flower of 30 petals, with its golden stamens, rich scent and the name of Le Roi Soleil. In his most recent catalogue, Peter Beales says of the colour it is so deep that it is almost black. 'Louis XIV' is a China rose and as such, somewhat tender and small, although with care it can still be used in a flower border with other shrubs, or as a specimen rose. Its ideal setting is a cool greenhouse or a conservatory, especially as the stems have so few thorns.

Between 1752 and 1824 the introduction into Europe of just four new roses, known as the stud Chinas, radically expanded the flowering period and colour range of roses in the second half of the nineteenth century and entirely changed the public perception of roses throughout the twentieth century. Many people still think of Hybrid Teas and Floribundas as the only roses suitable for most gardens. These two classes were not just modern but ubiquitous, for a while excluding nearly everything that had gone before.

The small group of China roses just preceded and to some extent overlapped this revolution. The Guillot nursery introduced 'Louis XIV' eight years before the first Hybrid Tea rose, which Guillot Fils called 'La France'.

The Guillot dynasty of rose-breeders is today in its fifth generation. The first was Jean-Baptiste Guillot. He set up his nursery near Lyons in 1829 and introduced some 80 new roses. His son of the same name introduced a further 79 cultivars with unashamedly grand titles. Identifying his deep crimson China rose with the Sun King, he allied its beauty with the great age of French literature and art, the splendid palaces of the late seventeenth century and especially Versailles.

The entrance to the Roseraies Guillot, Lyon Montplaisir, in the early 1900s.

class: **Bourbon**
date: **1880**
grower: **Garçon**
flower: **very double**
colour: **deep pink/magenta**
scent: **raspberry/nectarine**
height: **1.8 metres**

Madame Isaac Pereire

Some of the finest roses have appeared on the market even as the fashion for their kind has suffered a steep decline. Hybrid Perpetuals were already supplanting the Bourbon roses of the early nineteenth century when, in 1851, Jules Margottin, a nurseryman of Bourg-la-Reine near Paris, introduced 'Louise Odier', a lilac-pink Bourbon of near perfect geometric shape and superb fragrance. For a century and a half, this fine rose has held its place in the catalogues of specialist rose nurseries, in defiance of the fact that its class is now reduced to a tenth of the cultivars which existed in the 1840s.

Margottin had probably given up much hope of there ever being another Bourbon so evidently first-rate when, in 1880, he noticed one bred in the nursery of Garçon of Rouen, entered in Garçon's catalogue as 'Le Bienheureux de la Salle' ('Blessing of the Bower'). Having seen this rose in flower, Margottin promptly enlisted the help of one of his customers, the wife of a rich Parisian banker and financier of the railways; with a little venture capital from Madame Isaac Pereire, he bought the rights to Garçon's rose and changed its name to honour her.

'Madame Isaac Pereire' has the largest blooms of any Bourbon: huge saucer-shaped flowers, deep pink-clouded magenta, the petals rolled and quartered and with a powerful raspberry and nectarine-like fragrance. Not surprisingly, it had many admirers in Victorian England, but the judges of rose shows during the Edwardian era condemned the entire plant for its 'coarse shape' and 'quite indefensible contour'. When the talented rosarian Foster-Melliar died (*see* 'Rambling Rector' p.74) leading officers of the National Rose Society deleted the offender from recommendation in the last edition of his *Book of the Rose* (1910). Today the Royal NRS has corrected a hasty judgment. 'Madame Isaac Pereire' is a fine pillar rose and much else besides. Provided the longest stems are pruned by a third of their length in winter, and attention is paid to cutting away all short and twiggy growth as soon as this has flowered, this rose will produce new shoots and flower into September, when the blooms are at their best.

'A Bourbon can usually be found to fulfil any role asked of it in the modern garden', writes Peter Beales (*Classic Roses*, 1997). Yet with the exception of Zéphirine Drouhin, Bourbon roses have been undervalued over the years. They mix well with all other old roses and their often powerful, somewhat damask-like fragrance matches their magnificent flowers.

class: **Damask**
date: **1830**
grower: **Marest**
flower: **very double**
colour: **blush-white**
scent: **sandalwood**
height: **1.3 metres**

Madame Zöetmans

In common parlance, all dark Roses are Damask, probably the first dark varieties having borne this name. But this is erroneous. There are dark Roses belonging to almost every group, and there are Damask Roses of various colours: some are white.

(*The Rose Garden* by William Paul)

'Madame Zöetmans' is one such rose, 'a delicate fresh colour changing to white, the many petals densely filling the sumptuous flowers'. The formation of these blush-white petals is that unique to old roses: the flower sometimes appears quartered with a 'button-eye' at the centre. This is an excellent rose for close admiration and is small enough for almost any garden or patio. Its only rival is the better-known 'Madame Hardy', a Damask rose with larger flowers that are pure white. Both are very fragrant: the scent of 'Madame Zöetmans' is sandalwood with a hint of lemon.

Paul's *The Rose Garden*, which popularised the White Damasks, was first published in 1848, went through nine editions and remains in print today. No writer on gardening was so widely studied in his lifetime. He issued hints for 'Villa Gardening', brochures for the less well-off on 'Roses and Rose Cultivation' and gave lectures on topics ranging from Brussels sprouts to 'American Plants, their History and Culture'. Even the great Darwin was in awe of his practical knowledge. Paul, who started his own nursery in Waltham Cross, north of London, in 1860, was one of the first plantsmen to receive the prestigious Victoria Medal of Honour of the Royal Horticultural Society and was, of course, elected a Fellow of the Linnaean Society.

Reading so keen an advocate of gardening inspires the planting of rare cultivars like 'Madame Zöetmans'. With its evocation of innocence, this rose makes an ideal present at the celebration of the naming of a child. Offer the flower with a quotation from the Bengali poet and philosopher Rabindranath Tagore's *Gitanjali*, the words beginning: 'The sleep that flits on baby's eyes – does anybody know from whence it comes?'

But first remove the thorns.

class: **Hybrid Musk**
date: **1924**
grower: **Pemberton**
flower: **semi-double**
colour: **creamy pink**
scent: **rich musk**
height: **1.5 metres**

Penelope

'Penelope' is universally acknowledged as a fine rose for having nearly every desirable attribute: the foliage is full, its dark green leaves broad and ribbed, the stems growing to shrub height of 1.5 metres. Large semi-double flowers are carried in small and large clusters and open to a creamy pink which offsets the stronger salmon-orange of other buds about to open. The petals are frilled at their edges; their scent combined with fragrance from the stamens, is distinctly musk and hangs on the air. After the flowers, the hips are whitened by a bloom on their surface, which softens their colour as it changes from cool green to coral pink.

The Hybrid Musk roses have their origin in the expertise of the Reverend Joseph Pemberton. From childhood, roses had enthralled him. On being sent to boarding school he combated his homesickness by preserving in a barley-sugar tin each year, a bloom of 'Souvenir de la Malmaison' from his parents' garden. Although the flower disintegrated during the autumn term, its sweet smell lingered until he could return home for the joys of Christmas.

Pemberton was renowned for the respect he showed towards his gardeners who, in addition to growing his beloved show roses, shared his determination to breed new cultivars of what he liked to call a 'small man's rose'. These possess two fundamental qualities: a flowering period extending from summer well into autumn and a lingering musk fragrance. Two of the gardeners Pemberton employed, Spruzen and Bentall, went on to found their own nurseries. They helped him to raise between 5,000 and 10,000 seedlings annually under glass. To achieve his aims Pemberton crossed various roses with 'Trier', a rose bred in the nursery of Peter Lambert in Germany. Although not particularly striking, this rose had strongly captured both the autumn-flowering nature and powerful fragrance of the ancient Musk rose, along with those same characteristics from the China and Multiflora roses of the Far East.

Between 1913 and his death in 1926, Pemberton was responsible for about two-dozen wonderful varieties, with names of classical resonance: The finest of this class are: 'Pax' (1918), 'Prosperity' (1919), 'Vanity' (1920), 'Francesca' (1922), 'Nur Mahal' (1923), 'Penelope' (1924) and 'Cornelia' (1925). All these roses require only light pruning and thinning of the old wood to retain vigour.

class: **Damask**

date: **1817**

grower: **Vibert**

flower: **double**

colour: **blush-pink**

scent: **warm musk**

height: **0.9 metres**

Petite Lisette

This is a shrub of downy grey-green foliage, with delightful sprays of blush-pink flowers and the strong warm fragrance of a true Damask rose. The petals open to perfection, revealing the formation of a button-eye at the centre of the flower. 'Petite Lisette', as its name implies, is ideal for a small garden or the front of a flower border.

This rose was introduced in 1817 by Jean-Pierre Vibert, a soldier wounded during Napoleon's campaign in Italy, who went on to become the leading rose specialist of France and the producer of 600 new cultivars. His confidence in his work is well illustrated by the wry boast he made to a colleague as he prepared for export the very fine rose named after his daughter Aimée: 'the English when they see it will go down on their knees'. It is possible they did and certainly they still do, but contrary to appearances Vibert was not a lone horticultural genius.

The Empress Josephine's insatiable demand for new roses had greatly benefitted the business of Jean Descemet, a nurseryman of St Denis. Descemet's production of about 80 new cultivars indicates he was the first grower to practise controlled crossbreeding, and for this purpose he kept careful records. He was in possession of some 300 cultivars and 10,000 seedlings when, in 1815, English troops marched on Paris. Aware that his political sympathies placed him in danger, Descemet decided to sell up and flee to Odessa. In Vibert he found a willing purchaser, ready to take custody of the precious notebooks and to transport the entire plant stock to the safety of Chennevières-sur-Marne. The troops did not fail to ransack the St Denis site. A few years later Vibert moved the entire nursery yet again, this time to the more favourable climate of Angers.

To what extent then do 'Petite Lisette' and the many fine roses of Vibert in fact owe their origin to the Empress Josephine and the skill of Descemet? The essential documents having, as far as we know, been lost, we can only guess.

class: **Damask**

date: **grown before 1689**

grower: **unknown**

flower: **semi-double**

colour: **pink**

scent: **spice**

height: **1.5 metres**

Professeur Emile Perrot

The rose grown not for its beauty but for its oil content is named in honour of Emile Perrot, author of *Plantes médicinales de France* (1928–38). This rose is also known as *Rosa X damascena* 'Trigintipetala', and sometimes called 'Kazanlik', after a Bulgarian town in the upper Toundja, which is situated amid 2,000 hectares of rose fields.

The spice-scented flowers of 'Professeur Emile Perrot' are harvested over a period of four weeks in late spring, from dawn to mid-morning, before the heat of the sun over the Toundja valley lowers the oil content of the petals. Two hectares of roses produces in excess of 1,200,000 blooms, weighing four tons; heated in stills of up to 2,000 litres capacity, this quantity yields one kilo of pure oil. Although a teaspoonful can cost £50, the demand for genuine oil has never been so great (*see* Appendix 1 p.88).

The physician, Avicenna (980–1037) is credited with the invention of the distillation of rose oil, but it seems to have been normal practice in Iran as early as the ninth century. The product was exported to China and India, until rivalled in the fifteenth century by output from the rose fields of Peshawar, in what is now Pakistan.

According to legend, the production of rose oil in India began in 1612. Soon after her marriage to the Mogul Emperor Jehangir Khan, the Princess Nur Mahal was being rowed in the heat of the day on a lake strewn with rose blossom. She dipped a piece of cotton into the water to absorb the film that appeared on the surface, and was amazed at how it retained the scent of the roses. Fields of roses were then planted by the Ganges at Ghazipur, where the liquid distilled from the petals was stored in sunken tanks. In the cool of morning, the oil would be collected by drawing a feather across the surface. Allowed to settle in sunlight, this oil changes from hazy green to clear amber, and can then be poured into phials.

During the seventeenth century, perfume manufacture developed at Grasse in France, where it continues today. Here, flower oils are extracted by a process known as *enfleurage*, in which petals are saturated in lard or some similar compound, which is then dissolved in alcohol to separate the oil. The oil extracted from roses by this method is called 'Rose Absolut'. At a height of 400 metres, the fields around Grasse are ideal ground for roses and other scented plants, including violets, mimosa, carnations and jasmine.

class: **Multiflora Rambler**

date: **prior to 1912**

grower: **unknown**

flower: **semi-double**

colour: **creamy white**

scent: **clove/musk**

height: **6 metres**

Rambling Rector

This friendly monster belongs to the category of super-charged ramblers called 'scramblers' by Peter Beales, the specialist grower of old roses at Attleborough in Norfolk. The scramblers go to great lengths, this one to about 6 metres, to colonise surrounding territory; the most 'vigorous', as gardeners like to say, is 'Kiftsgate', which Beales assesses at 9 metres, although many will argue that even this is an understatement.

Having described 'Rambling Rector' as friendly, it is a monster nonetheless to anyone who tries to force a way through its thorny mound; this makes it an excellent sentinel on the remote boundaries of a garden. The most common use for 'Rambling Rector' is as a cloak for eyesores: ruined sheds, old privies, corrugated iron-clad cesspits, trees butchered by cowboy pruning or walls which simply look ugly. All these can be improved by its grey-green downy foliage. In early summer this rose is a cascade of clove and musk-scented milk-cream flowers with creamy yellow centres. In autumn it provides a multitude of little yellow hips.

No one seems to know how 'Rambling Rector' was first propagated or which cleric it called to mind. Dean Hole, author of the extremely rambling *Book about Roses* (1869) was an entertaining Victorian rosarian but vicar, not rector, of Caunton. The Reverend Joseph Pemberton, the author of *Roses* (1908), wrote so well it would be unfair to cite him, likewise the clerical garden journalist Shirley Hibberd (1825–1890). My vote goes to Andrew Foster-Melliar, the rector of Sproughton and author of *The Book of the Rose* (1894), 'a great talker' at the rose shows but who otherwise had little else to say: his parishioners once begged him to make his sermons longer. His son draws this amusing picture of him in the rectory garden:

> …the trout pool hidden beneath the old elm and among the roses, was one of his pleasures. There on summer evenings, he would sit for hours feeding the fat trout with bread and earwigs, the latter of which he would blow onto the water by means of hollow tubes.
>
> (*Memoir of Andrew Foster-Melliar*, 1910)

class: **Species Rambler**
date: **est. 15 million years**
grower: **unknown**
flower: **single**
colour: **pale pink**
scent: **musk**
height: **3 metres**

Rosa Canina

The Dog Rose is so common in the countryside that it often escapes attention. We notice this wild briar when the long prickly stems show traceries of small rose-pink flowers or red hips. We may know where there are heaps of it along a particular route, as on the M40 north of Banbury. For a mile or so the northbound and southbound carriageways divide and a central island sprouts thickets of *R. canina*. Our curiosity is aroused at the sight of what looks, at a distance, like a mass of glistening foam. The heart lifts at the realisation that this is a sea of roses. The flowers have a soft 'rose' scent from their five petals and a hint of musk from their stamens.

The Dog Rose was thought to be an antidote to rabies, hence its name. It turned out to be a somewhat less powerful medicine, a valuable source of vitamin C. During the Second World War and afterwards, when there was food rationing in the UK, there was a vital national campaign for dosing children with William Ransome's Rose-Hip Syrup, to make up for a shortage of fresh fruit and salad. You could not eat the hips raw as their seeds inside were covered with irritating white hairs which were bitter to the taste. They made your tongue curl. An adaptation of Marguerite Patten's recipe for the sweet rose-hip syrup goes as follows:

Coarsely grate or chop 1lb of rosehips and immediately put them into 3 pints of boiling water. Simmer for five minutes then let stand for 15 minutes. Strain the juice through layers of fine muslin and add 8–12oz [200–300g, 4–6 US cups] of sugar to each pint. Heat and stir well. As soon as the sugar dissolves cease boiling. Pour the hot syrup into hot jars with well-fitting screw-top lids. Lid when cool. Keep refrigerated and use within two months.

The protagonist of the informal garden style, William Robinson, condemned 'the monotony and barrenness of rosaries' and went on to suggest planting Dog Roses, 'by grass walks or rough banks or in newly-made hedgerows'. I cannot agree with him wholeheartedly. My own preferred constituents for the planting of a country hedge are: lots of blackthorn, some hazel, an occasional spindle, some Sweet Briar definitely, a Dog Rose perhaps, and honeysuckle. This blend of wilderness will offer snowdrifts of flowers in spring, greenery and fragrant flowers in summer, fiery embers in autumn and food and shelter for wildlife in winter.

class: **Gallica**

date: **ancient**

grower: **unknown**

flower: **semi-double**

colour: **light crimson**

scent: **floral/light musk**

height: **I metre**

Rosa Gallica Officinalis

The Apothecary's Rose, in Latin *Rosa officinalis*, is also the Red Rose of Lancaster and the Rose of Provins. The foliage is dark grey-green, the flower light crimson with golden yellow stamens, and sweetly-scented. The petals, more than those of any other rose, retain their fragrance when dried and reduced to a powder. For centuries this made them invaluable for use in medicinal unguents and potions.

In Persia the rose was fully exploited as a source of medicine and as a prophylactic. An industry centred on Shiraz produced the rose-water known as julep; the caliph of Baghdad received annually 30,000 bottles of the 'essence of red roses'. The dealer in perfumes, the Al Attar, was licensed like a modern pharmacist to make up prescriptions which included crushed petals and attar, the oil of roses. Baghdad under Islamic rule supported numerous perfumeries, 27,000 public baths, and bathed all its hospital patients by order twice a week. Extracts of rose in clay soap and rose-water played an essential part in all aspects of hygiene.

By the thirteenth century a small industry, centred on the town of Provins south-east of Paris, found the local climate particularly favourable for growing *R. gallica* var. *officinalis*. Apothecaries there compounded the flowers for use in medicinal jams and ointments. About the same time this red rose was adopted as an emblem by Edmund Crouchback, the first Earl of Lancaster, the second son of Henry III of England and Eleanor of Provence: the heraldic badges of red and white roses predate the Wars of the Roses by 200 years. The emblem, which became the Red Rose of England, was the same *R. gallica* var. *officinalis* used in liniments applied to the wounds of war.

By the fourteenth century, apothecaries could obtain classical and Arab medical texts published by the Benedictine monks of Solerno. Over the next three centuries apothecaries throughout France and England were regulated by laws governing their education and trading. In France all potions and embrocations had to be labelled and dated, including extracts of the Apothecary's Rose. Anyone caught selling stale goods was fined 50 livres and had their stock burned in the shop doorway. Putrid rose-petals could ruin a business.

Rosa Mundi

According to the sixteenth-century chronicler John Stow, an early mention of 'Rosa Mundi' (*Rosa gallica* 'Versicolor') appeared in an epitaph on the lost tomb of Rosamund Clifford, the mistress of Henry II, who was buried at a nunnery in Godstowe near Oxford:

> Hic jacet in tumba Rosa Mundi, non Rosa Munda
>
> Non redolet, sed olet, quae redolere solet.

The King was reputed to have built Fair Rosamund a palace at Woodstock called the Labrynthus: 'wrought like unto a knot in a garden, called a maze … a house of wonderful working so that no man or woman could come to her but that was instructed by the King'. Henry had evidently been reading Theseus and the Minotaur. His ingenious scheme, however, did not foil the jealous wife, whose knowledge of the Greek myth lacked no eye for detail. Queen Eleanor found her way to Rosamund 'by clue of a thridde or silk, and so dealt with her that she lived not long after'. The Queen's supporters evidently wrote the epitaph. In fair translation it reads:

> Here the rose graced, not the rose chaste, reposes;
>
> The scent that rises is no scent of roses.

There exists no more definite an account of 'Rosa Mundi' in the medieval period. Not until 1581 does Matthew de L'Obel (after whom lobelia is named) describe what could be the elusive rose, as do three herbalists after him: Clusius, Besler and Caspar Bauchin. *The Garden Book of Sir Thomas Hanmer* (1659) states categorically that 'Rosa Mundi' was 'first found in Norfolk a few years since upon a branch of the common red rose'. 'Rosa Mundi' is indeed a striped sport of the Apothecary's Rose, though it is reasonable to assume that such a stunning flower would have generated many more references than Stow's imaginative tale had it been widely grown in medieval Britain.

The gardeners at Castle Howard in Yorkshire tell of a 'Rosa Mundi' not so long ago that escaped and suckered its way for hundreds of yards across the lawns. Try how they might they could not stop it. Despite its vigour and a weakness for mildew, 'Rosa Mundi' is a popular shrub of cottage gardens because of its very large semi-double flowers produced in great quantity, even on poor soil. Its old rose fragrance is as intoxicating in reality as it is in legend.

class: **Rugosa**
date: **before 1940**
grower: **unknown**
flower: **single**
colour: **silvery-cerise**
scent: **clove/curd**
height: **1.8 metres**

Scabrosa

The Rugosa roses are tough, thrive on sandy soils and make excellent hedges, particularly in windswept seaside areas and on the islands of motorways. They can be pruned after flowering but only at the loss of their hips, which grow to the size of small tomatoes except in the sterile form. These are particularly good for making jams and syrups (for a syrup recipe, see 'Rosa Canina', p.76). The large flowers of the Rugosas do not open all at once but over a long period, so it is often the case that in autumn late flowers appear alongside the ripe hips. The scent of these flowers is like that of Gallica or Damask roses but with the addition of cloves, better – it has to be said – than cloves themselves. A pot pourri of Rugosa petals and mint is deeply calming.

I first encountered Rugosa roses with their stems of dense prickles when I was asked to dig up a row of them on a steep bank. Halfway through this exercise the neighbour on whose boundary they were situated complained. Following an exchange of views I was asked to put the roses back. This was impossible, as those that had been lifted were given away. I

spaced out the remaining Rugosas at intervals of a metre, which is as they should have been planted in the first place; so the morning's work was not entirely wasted. Allowing the circulation of air around roses and light to their leaves is as important as pruning and the soil in which they are set growing.

The first Rugosa to be grown in Europe came to Holland from Japan. It was called 'Ramanas', a gutteral mispronunciation of the Japanese 'Hama Nasi', meaning 'beach pear'. This rose was introduced into England as a novelty by the Hammersmith nursery of Lee and Kennedy in 1796 and was virtually ignored. Not until the end of the nineteenth century did the French nursery Cochet-Cochet lead a sudden rush to produce garden varieties. The unpleasantly named 'Scabrosa', meaning 'rough to the touch', is one of the most useful hybrids but no nursery seems to know who was the first to propagate it. Disease-resistant, except for rust, its foliage is thick even to ground level, the 14-cm silvery-cerise flowers are made especially beautiful by their prominent cream-coloured stamens.

class: **Hybrid Perpetual**
date: **1899**
grower: **Robichon**
flower: **double**
colour: **crimson striped pink**
scent: **floral/spice**
height:**1.2 metres**

Souvenir de Jeanne Balandreau

One of the great roses of the late nineteenth century is 'Ulrich Brunner Fils', which some years after its introduction in France produced a sport with striped flowers. Named in honour of someone whose identity is now a mystery, this sport, 'Souvenir de Jeanne Balandreau,' is one of the loveliest flowers of its kind: large, double and cupped, rich crimson striped pink, and very fragrant. The entire plant is well proportioned, with grey-green foliage and few thorns, it grows to a little more than a metre in height and is ideal for the patio.

Striped roses appealed to Victorian and later Edwardian taste, but have since enjoyed only

brief periods of popularity. Many varieties have been abandoned. There are now in nursery catalogues just three plants available from the list of ten striped Gallicas recommended in William Paul's *The Rose Garden* (1848): 'Mundi', 'Oeillet Parfait' and 'Perles des Panachées'. The 'Village Maid' of Paul's list probably refers to 'Centifolia Variegata', and missing from his list is the popular and highly fragrant 'Camaieux'.

A writer in the *Historic Roses Group Journal*, Brigid Quest-Ritson, recently complained at having to trudge around an entire nursery when trying to compare striped roses. She wistfully remembered a visit to Cavriglia in Italy where, in defiance of botanical classes, Professor Gianfranco Fineschi had displayed his striped roses all together for the benfit of visitors to his private garden. In pride of place, of course, was 'Variegata di Bologna', created by Bonfiglioli in 1909, and described as 'cream streaked with blackcurrant purée'. Peter Beales, in his *Classic Roses* (1985), is not so sure, 'reminding me', he says, 'of the semolina and blackcurrant jam of school dinner days'. 'Souvenir de Jeanne Balandreau', although not quite so striking, appeals by the size of its flowers.

'Variegata di Bologna': a scented Bourbon rose of fully double, cupped flowers with vivid crimson-purple stripes on a creamy-white background.

class: **Scots Rose**
date: **1838**
grower: **Lee**
flower: **very double**
colour: **blush pink**
scent: **Lily of the Valley**
height: **1.5 metres**

Stanwell Perpetual

The chance seedling of what appears to have been a cross between a wild Scots Rose and an Autumn Damask was found in a garden at Stanwell in Surrey and put onto the market by the old nursery of Lee in Hammersmith, London. Uniquely for a Scots Rose, this variety has consolidated from its second parent a tendency of repeat-flowering into late summer, hence the name, 'Stanwell Perpetual'. The shrub is 1.5 metres high; suckering, thorny, scrawny and yet graceful, its foliage glaucous-green. The sweet-scented double flower opens blush-pink and cupped, and extends nearly flat to a cream-flushed-pink bloom of exquisitely quilled and quartered petals and a button eye.

The old Scots Roses are varieties or cultivars of the low-growing Burnet Rose, in Latin *R. pimpinellifolia*, found suckering on coastal cliffs and hillsides over a wide area from Iceland to Siberia and throughout Europe. It seems not to mind the salt spray of the sea, or the brutal wind of the Burren in Ireland, where it nestles on the shattered limestone pavements. It has 'shutes, twigges and branches covered all over with thicke small thornie prickles', according to Dodonaeus' *Herbal* (1575): 'the flowers be small single and white, and of good savour', with a scent like that of Lily of the Valley.

In 1793, Robert Brown and his brother transplanted some varieties of this wild rose into their nursery from the hill of Kinnoul near Perth. Selecting from seedlings, they and other Scottish nurseries produced prior to 1830 over 200 single and double-flowered cultivars in colours ranging from white to crimson and yellow. Only four can now be identified from this early period and they are rare: 'Fulgens', 'Falkland', 'Loch Leven' and 'Staffa'.

This small group of roses continued to be expanded by cross-breeding and the introduction of new discoveries until the 1840s. Although highly recommended by Gertrude Jekyll for their informality, these old roses were almost overlooked throughout the twentieth century until a retired horticulturist and botanical artist, Mary McMurtrie, published her *Scots Roses* (1998).

Born in Skene, Aberdeenshire, in 1902, Mary has striven all her life to save and maintain old varieties of all manner of flowers. I last heard of her at the age of a hundred, living not far from the village of her youth, putting the finishing touches to her eagerly awaited book, *Flora of Scotland*.

Appendix 1: A Note on the Manufacture and Use of Rose Oil

The different extracts of roses used in perfumes and herbal remedies often give rise to confusion. Potential buyers of rose oil might wonder, for instance, why Rose Absolut is half the price of Rose Otto, and what else distinguishes these products.

The first distinction to be aware of is how the type of rose itself, the class even more than the variety, can affect the cost of the product. Broadly speaking, the yield from Centifolia roses is high, but not of the finest quality. The yield from Damask roses is low but high in quality, hence the widespread use of the Damask rose 'Trigintipetala', otherwise known as 'Professeur Emile Perrot' ('Kazanlik'), for high-quality rose oil.

Rose Absolut is obtained by the use of a solvent to extract the oil from the petals. This is achieved at no risk to the stability of the fragrance but the end product inevitably bears traces of the organic solvent. Rose Otto, on the other hand, is pure rose oil obtained by means of distillation. This process involves the use of heat and consequently the fragrance of the oil is disturbed. The purity of Rose Otto, however, makes it the preferred choice for medicinal use.

Rose tinctures and rose-waters contain a small proportion of rose oil. The best tinctures are obtained by serial use of more than one extraction method on the petals, in order to retain certain of the non-volatile elements of the rose. These trace elements enhance the product's therapeutic value.

The various forms of rose oil, tinctures and rose-waters are used as a liver-tonic and are also anti-viral. They are employed as 'the female remedy supreme', helping to regulate periods and mitigate the effects of the menopause. In times of severe stress and bereavement, rose oil and rose tincture is comforting and uplifting, both act upon the body as an astringent. Rose oil is often used to counterbalance the more aggressive herbs in a prescription.

Appendix 2: A Note on Planting and Pruning

Old roses are not difficult to grow and guidance on their cultivation can be found in the one-volume *RHS Encyclopedia of Gardening*. The following note of advice on planting and pruning is to help the first-time grower to get started.

Remember that the oldest roses – Albas, Gallicas, Centifolias, Damasks and Ramblers – are once-flowering only. Apart from their delightfully informal habits of growth and sometimes splendid autumn hips, the unique charm of their flowers is compensation for brevity in this respect. One-third of the roses featured in this book last longer: the Noisette and the Rugosa roses are repeat-flowering, whilst the Portland, the Bourbon, the China, the Hybrid Perpetuals and the Hybrid Musks flower continuously in the summer months. Among Scots Roses, 'Stanwell Perpetual' is the only one which flowers more than once.

Roses for the garden should normally be ordered from a nursery in early summer, for delivery bare-rooted in November. In the event of a delay between their arrival and planting, they can be temporarily 'heeled in' to a trench so that the roots are not out of the ground should there be a dry wind or a frost. Roses in plastic containers may be planted at any time of the year, except when the ground is frozen. For ecological reasons, the National Trust does not recommend the buying of any plants sold in peat-based compost.

Dig over the ground where a rose is to be planted to a depth of half a metre and a width of one metre, at the same time adding some well-decayed farmyard manure and a couple of handfuls of bonemeal. Under no circumstances plant a rose where a rose has been growing, unless the soil has been replaced or rested for three years.

Before planting a bare-rooted rose, first trim any of the very long roots. Then make a small mound of soil in the planting-hole to rest the rose on, as the soil is pushed back in and pressed moderately firm. The union of the rose, where the shoots and roots join, should be a little below the surface (25mm) once the hole is filled to ground level. In early spring, spread a layer of medium-fine bark or other organic mulch over the soil to keep the roots cool and moist.

Old roses grown as shrub roses should be hard-pruned after planting to force new shoots from the base. Thereafter, the oldest – Albas, Gallicas, Damasks and Centifolias – may be left alone, their stems supported where necessary, or lightly pruned according to the suggestions given in the Introduction. Hybrid Perpetuals, Hybrid Musks and Portland Roses benefit from fairly hard pruning in February. This involves cutting out thin or overcrowded growth, reducing the main shoots by a third and the remainder by two-thirds. Bourbon Roses are best pruned lightly, shaping the shrub and removing any overcrowded wood at the centre.

Ramblers flower on the previous year's growth. If for some reason they have to be cut back, this should be done just after the flowering. However, if the intention is to remove very old stems which are past their best, wait until winter when the rose is dormant. Noisettes, and Hybrid Perpetuals trained as climbers, produce flowers on the same year's growth. Their long shoots should be trained in as many directions as possible and the lateral shoots cut to a third of their length after flowering each year. Occasionally, a strong lateral may be spared to become a main shoot. Scots Roses should be left alone, except for a very hard pruning after several years, when they have become too straggly.

Dead-heading flowers that have died off is usually a good practice. Cut above the second or third leaf below the truss or flower stem, but do not dead-head roses which produce colourful hips.

Gardens with Old Roses

Tourist Information Offices generally maintain full details of opening times. Before visiting, it is also advisable to contact the Garden Manager's office, as flowering times vary and the season is short.

(S) indicates opening restricted mainly to Sunday afternoons in summer.

Arley Hall, nr Northwich, Cheshire

Birmingham University Botanic Garden, Winterbourne

Broughton Castle, Banbury, Oxfordshire

Castle Howard, North Yorkshire

Cranborne Manor, Cranborne, Dorset

Crathes Castle (NTS) Aberdeenshire

Dixon Park, Belfast, Northern Ireland

Drum Castle (NTS), Aberdeenshire

Elsing Hall, East Dereham, Norfolk (S)

Gardens of the Rose (RNRS), St Albans, Hertfordshire

Greys Court (NT), Henley-on-Thames, Oxfordshire

Haddon Hall, Bakewell, Derbyshire

Ham House (NT) Richmond-upon-Thames, London (small 17th-century collection)

Hardwick Hall (NT), nr Chesterfield, Derbyshire

Helmingham Hall, nr Ipswich, Suffolk (S)

Hidcote Manor Garden (NT), nr Chipping Camden, Gloucestershire

Hinton Amper Garden (NT), Bramdean, nr Alresford, Hampshire

Hyde Hall (RHS), Chelmsford, Essex

Kellie Castle (NTS), Pittenweem, Fife

Kiftsgate Court, nr Chipping Camden, Gloucestershire

Leeds Castle, Maidstone, Kent

Malleny House Gardens (NTS), Balerno, Edinburgh

Mannington Hall, Saxthorpe, nr Norwich, Norfolk

Montacute House (NT), Somerset

Mottisfont Abbey (NT), nr Romsey, Hampshire (National Collection of Old Roses)

Mount Stewart (NT), Newtownards, Northern Ireland (limited collection)

Nymans Garden (NT), Haywards Heath, West Sussex

Oxford University Botanic Garden, Oxford

Polesden Lacey (NT), nr Dorking, Surrey

Pound Hill, West Kington, Wiltshire

Powis Castle (NT), Welshpool, Powys

Queen Mary Rose Gardens, Regents Park, London.

Rowallane Garden (NT), Co. Down, Northern Ireland (limited collection)

Royal Botanic Gardens, Kew, London

Sheldon Manor, Chippenham, Wiltshire.

Sissinghurst Castle Garden (NT), Cranbrook, Kent

Sudeley Castle, Winchcombe, Gloucestershire

The Manor, Hemingford Grey, Cambridgeshire

Time Trail of Roses, Wells, Somerset (S)

Waddesdon Manor, nr Aylesbury, Buckinghamshire

List of Suppliers

UK

Peter Beales Roses, London Road, Attleborough, Norfolk NR17 1AY
Tel: 01953 454707   Fax: 01953 456845
www.classicroses.co.uk
E-mail: sales@classicroses.co.uk

David Austin Roses Ltd, Bowling Green Lane, Albrighton, Shropshire WV7 3HB
Tel: 01902 376300   Fax: 01902 372142
www.davidaustinroses.com
E-mail: retail@davidaustinroses.co.uk

Scotts Nurseries Ltd, Merriott, Somerset TA16 5PL
Tel: 01460 72306   Fax: 01460 77433

Acton Beauchamp Roses, nr Worcester, WR6 5AE
Tel: 01531 640433   Fax: 01531 640802

Hunt's Court Garden Nursery, North Nibley, Dursley, Gloucestershire GL11 6DZ
Tel: 01453 547440   Fax: 01453 549944
E-mail: keith@huntscourt.fsnet.co.uk

Cranborne Manor Garden Centre, Cranborne, Dorset BH21 5PP
Tel: 01725 517248   Fax: 01725 517862
www.cranborne.co.uk
E-mail: gardencentre@cranborne.co.uk

Wych Cross Nurseries & Garden Centre, Forest Row, East Sussex RH18 5JW
Tel: 01342 822705   Fax: 01342 825329
www.wychcross.co.uk
E-mail: roses@wychcross.co.uk

Dairy Farm Nursery & Rose Centre, Bramford, nr Ipswich, Suffolk IP8 4JT
Tel: 01473 833359   Fax: 01473 833677
www.dairy-farm-nursery.co.uk
E-mail: sales@dairy-farm-nursery.co.uk

Seale Nurseries, Seale Lane, Seale, Farnham, Surrey GU10 1LD
Tel: 01252 782410   Fax: 01252 783038
www.sealsuperroses.com
E-mail: roses@sealsuperroses.com

Frampton Roses, 34 Dorchester Road, Frampton, Dorchester, Dorset DT2 9NF
Tel: 01300 320453

Wisley Plant Centre (RHS), Woking, Surrey GU23 6QB
Tel: 01483 211113   Fax: 01483 212372
www.rhs.org.uk
E-mail: wisleyplantcentre@rhs.org.uk

Mottisfont Abbey Garden Shop, Mottisfont, nr Romsey, Hampshire SO51 0LP
Tel: 01794 341901   Fax: 01794 341492
E-mail: mottisfontabbey@ntrust.org.uk

Castle Howard Garden Shop, Castle Howard, North Yorkshire YO60 7DA
Tel: 01653 648444   Fax: 01653 648501
www.castlehoward.co.uk

AUSTRALIA

Walter Duncan Roses, The Rose Garden Ltd, PO Box 18, Watervale, SA 5452
Tel: 08 8843 4000   Fax: 08 8843 4044
E-mail: wdroses@capri.net.au

Ross Roses, St Andrews Terrace, Willunga, SA 5172
Tel: 08 8556 2555   Fax: 08 8556 2955
www.rossroses.com.au
E-mail: orders@rossroses.com.au

BELGIUM

Pépinières Louis Lens s.a., Redinnestraat 11, 8460 Oudenburg
Tel: 059 267 830   Fax: 059 265 614
www.lens-roses.com
E-mail: info@lens-roses.com

CANADA

Pickering Nurseries Inc., 670 Kingston Road, Pickering, ONT. LIV 1A6
Tel: 905 839 2111   Fax: 905 839 4807
www.pickeringnurseries.com

FRANCE

Pépinières Loubert, Les Brettes, 49350 Les Rosiers-sur-Loire
Tel: 02 41 518082/06 87 035880   Fax: 02 41 380602
E-mail: therese.loubert@wanadoo.fr

Roseraie Guillot, Domaine de la Plaine, 38460 Chamagnieu
Tel: 04 74 902755   Fax: 04 74 902717
www.rosesguillot.com
E-mail: guillot@rosesguillot.com

Les Roses Anciennes de André Eve, ZA Morailles, 45308 Pithiviers, Cedex
Tel: 02 38 300130   Fax: 02 38 307165
www.roses-anciennes-eve.com
E-mail: info@roses-anciennes-eve.com

GERMANY

Rosen von Schultheis, 61231 Bad Nauheim, Steinfurth
Tel: 06032 81013   Fax: 06032 85890
www.rosenhof-schultheis.de
E-mail: bestellen@rosenhof-schultheis.de

List of Suppliers

SWITZERLAND

Richard Huber AG, Baumschulen, 5605 Dottikon
Tel: 056 624 18 27   Fax: 056 624 24 24
www.rosen-huber.ch
E-mail: bestellungen@rosen-huber.ch

HOLLAND

J.D. Maarse, Oosteinderweg 489, 1432 BJ Aalsmeer
Tel: 0297 324683   Fax: 0297 340597
www.maarse.nl
E-mail: Info@maarse.nl

ITALY

Il Giardino delle Rose di Maria Giulia Cimarelli, Via
Palastra 27, 50020 Chiesanuova, Florence
Tel/Fax: 055 82 42 388

Centro Botanico srl, Via G. De Grassi 15, 20123, Milan
Tel: 024 80 09 153   Fax: 024 81 96 636
www.centrobotanico.it
E-mail: centrobotanico@centrobotanico.it

NEW ZEALAND

Tasman Bay Roses, P.O. Box 159, Motueka
Tel/Fax: 03 528 7449
www.tbr.co.nz
E-mail: tbr@xtra.co.nz

Trevor Griffiths & Son, 304 Pages Road, Timaru
Tel/Fax: 03 686 1060

USA

Vintage Gardens, 2833 Old Gravenstein Highway South,
Sebastopol, CA 95472
Tel: 707 829 2035   Fax: 707 829 9516
www.vintagegardens.com

Roses of Yesterday and Today, 803 Brown's Valley Road,
Watsonville, CA 95076
Tel: 831 728 1901
www.rosesofyesterday.com

Antique Rose Emporium, 9300 Lueckemeyer Road,
Brenham, TX 77833-6453
Tel: 979 836 9051   Fax: 979 836 0928
www.weAREroses.com

Wayside Gardens, Hodges, South Carolina
Tel: 800 845 1124   Fax: 800 817 1124
www.waysidegardens.com

Heirloom Roses, 24602 Riverside Drive North-East,
St Paul, OR 97137

Tel: 503 538 1576   Fax: 503 538 5902
www.heirloomroses.com
E-mail: info@heirloomroses.com

Select Bibliography

AUSTIN, David, *Old Roses and English Roses* (1992)

BEALES, Amanda, *Old Fashioned Roses, Their Care and Cultivation* (1990)

BEALES, Peter, *Classic Roses* (1997 edition)

COX, Euan Hillhouse Methuen, *Plant-hunting in China* (1945)

Find that Rose (Published annually by the British Rosegrowers' Association)

GIBSON, Michael, *Shrub Roses, Climbers and Ramblers* (1981)

GRIFFITHS, Trevor, *Glorious Old Roses* (2000)

HARKNESS, Jack, *Roses* (1978)

Hillier Manual of Trees and Shrubs (1991)

Journals of the Historic Roses Group of the Royal National Rose Society (1991–2002)

JOYAUX, François, *La Rose de France* (1998)

JOYAUX, François, *La Rose, une Passion Française, Histoire de la Rose en France* 1778–1914 (2001)

KENNETT, Frances, *History of Perfume* (1975)

KRUSSMAN, Gerd, *Roses* (1982)

LE ROUGETEL, Hazel, *A Heritage of Roses* (1988)

McMURTRIE, Mary, *Scots Roses* (1998)

O'BRIAN, Patrick, *Joseph Banks* (1987)

PATERSON, Allen, *The History of the Rose* (1983)

PHILLIPS, Roger and RIX, Martyn, *The Quest for the Rose* (1993)

Rose Annuals of the Royal National Rose Society (1921ff)

ROSE, Graham, KING, Peter and SQUIRE, David, *The Love of Roses* (1990)

Royal Horticultural Society Encyclopedia of Gardening (1992)

Royal Horticultural Society Plant Finder (2002–2003)

SCARMAN, John, *Gardening with Old Roses* (1996)

SHEPHERD, Roy, *History of the Rose* (1954)

THOMAS, Graham Stuart, *The Graham Stuart Thomas Rose Book* (1994)

WILSON, Robert McNair, *Josephine* (1984)

YOUNG, Norman, *The Complete Rosarian* (1971)

Acknowledgements & Picture Credits

Thanks are due to Brenda Catherall, Barbara Mercer, Candida Boyes and John Sales for work on the text. To Maggie Tarbox at the Royal National Rose Society. To Ann Bird, Jim McIntyre and Robert Calkin of the Historic Roses Group. Guidance around the two largest collections of old roses at historic locations was kindly given by head gardener David Stone, at Mottisfont Abbey; head gardener Brian Deighton and gardener Christopher Stone at Castle Howard.